CAMBRIDGE STUDIES IN LATIN AMERICAN
AND IBERIAN LITERATURE

The politics of Spanish American *modernismo*

The politics of Spanish American modernismo elucidates the professional and literary means through which Spanish American *modernistas* negotiated a cultural politics of rapprochement with Spain and Europe in order to differentiate their Americanness from that of the United States. Gerard Aching argues that these turn-of-the-century men of letters were in fact responsible for the burgeoning role that intellectuals and writers had (and continue to have) in defining pan-Hispanism. Aching's arguments contribute to current debates about modernity and the colonial/postcolonial condition in nineteenth-century Hispanic literatures. The interdisciplinary approach will appeal to scholars in literature, cultural studies, Latin American studies, and history.

CAMBRIDGE STUDIES IN LATIN AMERICAN
AND IBERIAN LITERATURE

The politics
of Spanish American
modernismo

By exquisite design

GERARD ACHING

New York University

CAMBRIDGE
UNIVERSITY PRESS

PUBLISHED BY THE PRESS SYNDICATE OF THE UNIVERSITY OF CAMBRIDGE
The Pitt Building, Trumpington Street, Cambridge CB2 1RP, United Kingdom

CAMBRIDGE UNIVERSITY PRESS
The Edinburgh Building, Cambridge CB2 2RU, United Kingdom
40 West 20th Street, New York, NY 10011-4211, USA
10 Stamford Road, Oakleigh, Melbourne 3166, Australia

First published 1997

Printed in the United States of America

Typeset in Baskerville

Library of Congress Cataloging-in-Publication Data available

*A catalog record for this book is available from
the British Library*

ISBN 0-521-57249-5 hardback

Contents

Acknowledgments

It gives me great pleasure to acknowledge the members of my dissertation committee, Professors José Piedra, Jonathan Monroe, and Mary Gaylord, with respect and gratitude. I especially thank my advisor, John W. Kronik, for his knowledge, counsel, and integrity. I am grateful to Professor Sylvia Molloy for her comments and advice on the manuscript. I thank my copy editor, Katharita Lamoza, for her professionalism and patience. With respect to archives, the Benson Latin American Collection at the University of Texas at Austin proved unsurpassable. Last but not least, I would like to express my gratitude to family and friends in California, Canada, and the Caribbean for their constant support along the way. I am particularly indebted to my parents and to Catherine Lenfestey, Françoise Amato, and Cecelia Lawless for their affection and kindness.

1

A reevaluation of the
modernistas' detachment

At its most rudimentary, this study offers close readings of selected *modernista* texts in order to determine and interrogate specific connections between aesthetics and Spanish American cultural autonomy. According to most sources, *modernismo* began in 1888 with the publication of Rubén Darío's *Azul* and ended around 1916, the year this poet died.[1] However, the breadth and longevity of the debates in this field indicate the extent to which this literature and its criticism continue to provide, in conjunction with other registers of inquiry, a discourse on identity and difference. One of the most frequent points of deliberation within these debates concerns the degree of political consciousness that the *modernistas* exercised in the production and dissemination of literature about Spanish American and pan-Hispanic culture. It is both the traditional and the evolving configurations of this discussion about their cultural work that I term the politics of Spanish American *modernismo* and consider my principal interest in this book.

To appreciate the nature of these configurations, let us observe two relatively recent instances of the politicization or, borrowing from one of Nietzsche's titles, the "uses and disadvantages" of *modernismo,* and note how the literary movement and its criticism have been objectified in order to express national and transnational cultural agendas. In Nicaragua, where Darío was born, the Ministry of Culture published a collection of the poet's writings under the title of *Prosas políticas* (1982). Jorge Valle-Castillo's prologue to the collection reincarnated the poet in such a way that competing assessments of Darío and his works were placed at odds, thereby delineating ideological battle-lines in Nicaragua's recent civil war. He argued that Somoza's dictatorship never encouraged

1

an objective understanding of the poet and that this was the reason Darío had been converted into a marble monument. By contrast, Valle-Castillo claims, the Sandinistas popularized the poet by transforming him into "carne viva" [living flesh], a characterization that alludes as much to theology as it does to a profane and collective human struggle for change. His accusation falls short of critiquing the fact that the marble statue was one of the most idealized tropes in the movement's aesthetics and that such a monument erected in Darío's honor represents the poet's as well as *modernismo*'s successful incorporation into Nicaragua's national patrimony. In any case, the poet's legacy was so thoroughly foundational for Valle-Castillo's readers that it served as a *lingua franca* spoken and understood by opposing sides in a civil war.

Critical discussions about *modernismo* are also employed to evoke an utopian, transnational culture. For example, in stark contrast to Valle-Castillo's contentious analysis of the Nicaraguan situation, there are commentaries on the movement that describe and advocate Hispanic unity. At the closing ceremony of the International Conference on Spanish and Hispanoamerican Modernism (Córdoba, Spain, October 1985), Manuel Olivencia summed up his interest in *modernismo* as follows:

Como Comisario General de España para la Exposición Universal de 1992, me interesa sobre todo este fenómeno como un vínculo de unión entre los pueblos. Que se llame el "modernismo español e iberoamericano" viene a demostrar una vez más que es la cultura uno de los bienes del activo de nuestro patrimonio común, que somos una verdadera comunidad de pueblos: Iberoamérica; precisamente porque titulamos de una forma conjunta valores comunes como son los de nuestra Historia y, sobre todo, los de nuestra cultura. (p. 478)

[As Spain's General Commissioner for the 1992 Exposition, I am above all interested in this phenomenon as a unifying bond among peoples. That it may be called "Spanish and Ibero-American *modernismo*" comes to demonstrate once more that culture is one of the assets of our common patrimony, that we are a true community of peoples: Ibero-America; precisely because we title in like manner common values such as those of our History, and, above all, those of our culture.]

The International Conference offered critics the forum to voice their differences of opinion on *modernismo*. But in his closing statement, Olivencia made a conciliatory gesture in order to celebrate a shared Iberoamerican culture and history, thereby erasing the social antagonisms that informed and continue to inform that culture and history. The assumption that underlies Olivencia's speech is that a cultural discourse operates like a commodity within an economy that he calls the "patrimonio común." For Olivencia, this common patrimony belongs to a group of nations that supposedly share the same social values. Yet, as we have seen in Valle-Castillo's prologue, it is the negotiation of these social values and patrimony through rhetorical maneuvers and the selection of a literary style that gives the discourse on *modernismo* its conflictive edge. In short, aesthetic criteria work to express and determine political allegiances. Proof of this adage may be ascertained by the fact that *modernismo*'s literary history amply records attempts either to confirm or to check the movement's relevance to Spanish American societies – that is, to read its literature either programmatically as manifestations of a cultural agenda or symptomatically as an overindulgent art for art's sake.

Embedded in the polemics over what may be termed the movement's *escapist* or *evasive detachment* is an imposed anachronism in which certain critics have tended to juxtapose the *modernistas'* aloofness to contemporary notions of cultural work within liberal, democratic regimes. According to this line of reasoning, these poets and writers were deemed apolitical because they distanced themselves from autochthonous and popular cultural expressions; as producers of high art, they would not or could not define national culture. It is my intention to resemanticize this critical commonplace and speak of detachment as an assertive engagement, that is to say, as the will to embellish from a precise cultural and discursive location – "*arriba* y *afuera*" [above and outside], as Julio Ramos succinctly states (p. 209).

Before explaining in greater detail how embellishment constitutes an engagement, I would like to outline the coordinates of the conventional debate on the *modernistas'* escapist detachment, especially since this book presents a response to the weight of that tradition. In the following passage from his *Critical Approaches to Rubén Darío* (1974), Keith Ellis offers a familiar evaluation of this escapism:

From the late eighteenth century, the years preceding Independence, and throughout the period of social upheaval and readjustment during the first two-thirds of the nineteenth century, Spanish American literature and literary criticism tended to be identified closely with the social reality of the area. This tendency was challenged during the last third of the century by the attitude, promoted chiefly by Darío, of detachment from social questions. While Darío could write literature that demonstrated this detachment and while his own pronouncements and criticism suggested a new status for literature and put emphasis on the craft of literature, he could not decisively affect critical practice among his contemporaries. (p. 25)

Ellis's use of the word "challenge" infers that Darío and others were intent upon distancing themselves from society and the issues of their day. And proof of that avoidance seems to lie in Darío's and his followers' supposedly excessive dedication to "the craft of literature" or, by implication, to the intentional separation of an aesthetic practice from the society that gave rise to it. Even if one were to pursue a line of inquiry based on Ellis's conception of Darío's art, one need only peruse the pages of Darío's *Autobiografía* to note the shortcomings of this argument. As a well-known poet and journalist, Darío was sought out by presidents, generals, and other Central American dignitaries to act as composer, writer, and spokesman. Herein lies the official support for Darío's embellishment of and praises for specific Spanish American regimes. In Central America alone, presidents Rafael Zaldívar of El Salvador and Adán Cárdenas of Nicaragua employed Darío's literary and journalistic services to glorify their regimes and maintain public opinion in their favor (Concha, p. 29). Among his many tasks as spokesman/writer for those regimes, one of Darío's responsibilities included working on the plan for Central American union (Ellis, p. 11). At various points in his literary and journalistic career, the poet also took diplomatic appointments in Madrid, Paris, and Buenos Aires. In light of these activities, how and in what terms do critics contend that the *modernistas* evaded social issues?

The debate over detachment

According to the region's literary history, *modernismo* marked the beginning of a Spanish American self-reflection and the conscious literary elaboration of a cultural uniqueness. At the same time, the role of the movement's members in facilitating this awareness has remained subject to debate. Historical reasons partially explain this paradox. The process of political independence in Spanish America began in the second decade of the nineteenth century and ended when Spain lost its last overseas colonies to the United States in 1898. However, unlike the current tendency to associate the colonized and postcolonial nation with the subversive use or abrogation of the colonizers' tongue, the language and literary institutions that nineteenth-century Spanish American writers and poets employed to express cultural difference relied heavily on an expertise in academically correct and refined Spanish. Because of a disproportionate access to it, this language and its institutionalization in Spanish America readily facilitated a privileged class-determined participation in cosmopolitan discourses. Through such activities, the region's ruling classes vied for cultural parity – mostly with Spain – and for superiority over the United States. Historicized in this manner, Spanish American *modernismo* plied an unsteady course between a poetics of cultural *rapprochement* with Europe and a geopolitics of national and regional independence from Spain. Hence, faced with the enigma of a literature that defined its brand of Americanness by actively reclaiming a European heritage, observers found it difficult to reconcile the *modernistas'* declaration of cultural independence with a cosmopolitan penchant for literature from former colonizers.

This apparent contradiction is most comprehensible from the perspective of transnational class alliances and conflicts in the course of an "international" bourgeois revolution that embraced certain sectors of Latin American societies.[2] Through its literature, the *modernista* movement brought privileged groups in the region into a burgeoning intertextual commerce with similar reading constituencies in Spanish America, Europe, and the United States. Yet it must also be remembered that this new trade had powerful opponents. Spanish American *modernista* texts did not overtly attest to the conflict between the popular and monied classes to define the region as much as they described and represented the rifts between monopolistic oligarchies and a bourgeoisie that had begun to reap benefits from economic liberalism and international trade. In *modernista* texts, "aristocratic" valorizations of literature, such as those based on propriety and genealogical integrity of expression, were often juxtaposed to the much maligned bourgeois practice of reveling in such material "excesses" as the uncritical acquisition of cosmopolitan style in literature, decor, and dress. The conflict between these classes informed new albeit shifting cultural boundaries, or what Adam Sharman calls "una cultura de librecambio, en la que el modernismo hace las veces de signo cultural del liberalismo" [a free-trade culture in which *modernismo* acts as a cultural sign for liberalism] (p. 331). In other words, it can be argued that the *modernista* politics of cultural identity cannot be divorced from efforts to delineate and concretize class allegiances. With respect to such allegiances, it is not simply a question of shifts in taste from one kind of literature and literary production to another or the so-called introduction of modernity to preindustrial societies. *Modernista* discourses and their representations of class conflicts describe moments of transition and rupture so that it became possible for readers to imagine and employ a critical language about unique cultural origins and difference.

Let us examine the literary criticism that states the case for the *modernistas'* escapist detachment. *Modernismo's* first critics employed a discourse that melded a racial genealogy with class interests to chide the movement's members for their deviance from Spanish aesthetic and cultural traditions. In arguments against opening the Spanish American writing space to other literatures, the identification and dismissal of a seemingly arbitrary embellishment is deployed to defend Hispanic, cultural homogeneity. What is striking, for example, about the similarity between Juan Valera's critique of Darío's enjoyment of beauty and Leopoldo Alas's rejection of the North American "goce de bienes de pura sensualidad" [enjoyment of goods of pure sensuality] (Alas, p. 237) is their common allusion to the materiality and materialism of exquisite art objects. For Valera, it is this attention to refinement that makes Darío's *Azul* "afrancesado" [Frenchified]; for Alas, it is the rejection of an overdetermined materialism that promises to unite Spaniards and Spanish Americans in the face of an aggressive, North American, cultural hegemony. Both writers base their approach to *modernismo* on the a priori validation of Spanish national literature as the founding tradition of a collective Hispanic identity or *raza*.[3] Moreover, that they make this assumption employing a language that associates cultural identity with the consumption of material goods is no mere coincidence. When they refer to the *modernista* errancy from *la raza* in terms of pure versus deviant national and racial genealogies, Alas, Valera, and others also couch their objections in a critique of bourgeois culture.

Initial objections to *modernismo* as a pan-Hispanic discourse were not made by Spanish critics alone. One cannot systematically reduce critical debates on *modernismo* and cultural autonomy to a nationalistic or regionalistic Spanish/Spanish American opposition. In fact, Luis Monguió observes that the rejection of *modernista* cosmopolitanism proceeds mostly from Spanish American critics ("De la problemática del modernismo," p. 263). For instance, the competition to produce a literature worthy of the region's expanding cultural relations with Europe is evident in the stance that the Uruguayan intellectual, José Enrique Rodó, takes against *modernista* aesthetics. Rodó's interest in cultural reunification with Spain is almost always associated with his essay, *Ariel* (1900) – the most renowned work of symbolic defiance against the United States in Spanish American letters at that time; but his opposition to Darío's literary style in "Rubén Darío" also plays an important role in Rodó's pursuit of cultural reconciliation with Spain. Rodó's rejection of the *modernista* aesthetic is stated in his often-cited reference to Darío: "No es el poeta de América" [He is not America's poet] (*Obras completas*, p. 169). In full agreement with Alas's critique of the Parisian "pestes pegajosas" [contagious plagues] that Spanish American writers have adopted, Rodó provides evidence of what Emir Rodríguez Monegal calls the Uruguayan's "actitud antimodernista" [*antimodernista* attitude] (p. 1323). Writing to Alas (June 30, 1897), Rodó defines Spanish Americanism in terms of competing literary styles:

Otro de los puntos sobre los que quisiera hablar detenidamente a Vd. es el de mi modo de pensar en presencia de las corrientes que dominan nuestra *nueva* literatura americana. Me parece haberlo afirmado alguna vez: nuestra reacción antinaturalista es hoy muy cierta, pero muy candorosa; nuestro modernismo apenas ha pasado de la superficialidad. En América, con los nombres de *decadentismo* y *modernismo*, se disfraza a menudo una abominable escuela de trivialidad y frivolidad literarias: una tendencia que debe repugnar a todo espíritu que busque ante todo, en literatura, motivos para sentir y pensar. Los que hemos nacido a la vida literaria, después de pasados los *tiempos heroicos* del naturalismo, no aceptamos de su legado lo que nos parece una conquista definitiva; los que vemos en la inquietud contemporánea, en la actual renovación de las ideas y los espíritus algo más, mucho más, que ese prurito enteramente pueril de retorcer la frase y de jugar con las palabras, a que parece querer limitarse gran parte de nuestro decadentismo americano, tenemos interés en difundir un concepto completamente distinto del modernismo como manifestación de anhelos, necesidades y oportunidades de nuestro tiempo, muy superiores a la diversión candorosa de los que satisfacen con los logogrifos del decadentismo *gongórico* y las ingenuidades del decadentismo *azul.* (pp. 1323–4)

[Another of the points about which I would like to speak to you at length is that of my way of thinking amidst the currents that dominate our *new* American literature. It seems to me that I have affirmed it once: our anti-Naturalist reaction is today very certain, but very naïve; our modernism has barely gone beyond superficiality. In America, under the names *decadentism* and *modernism*, an abominable school of literary triviality and frivolity often disguises itself: a tendency that must repel every spirit that seeks above all, in literature, motives for feeling and thinking. Those of us who have been born to literary life, after Naturalism's heroic times, do not accept from its legacy what seems to us a definitive conquest; those of us who see in the contemporary yearning, in the current renewal of ideas and spirits something more, much more, than that entirely puerile urge to twist phrases and play with words, to which a great deal of our American decadentism wants to limit itself, are interested in disseminating a completely different concept of modernism as a manifestation of our times' long-ings, needs, and opportunities, far superior to the innocent pastime of those who satisfy with the enigmas of *Gongoric* decadentism and the naïvetés of *Azure* decadentism.]

In his indictment of *modernismo*, Rodó decries the movement's literary style for the same reasons that Valera, Alas, and others did: an obsessive interest in exquisite and embellishing referents. "These poets insist," observes Gwen Kirkpatrick, "on showing the physicality of the referent, shoving it to the forefront, as well as accentuating the physical nature of the words themselves" (p. 8).

Rodó repudiates the perceived ostentation of *modernista* aesthetics by associating it with an ethical and historical decadence. In his view, Spanish American *modernismo* is reminiscent of Góngora's work because they both represent periods of an overt materialism in decline. For Rodó and other critics who hold similar opinions of *modernismo*, the useless wordplay and overemphasis on (sculpting) the signifier – for Valera, a sure way to create "signos hueros" [empty signs] or an absence of meaning (*Obras completas 3*, p. 292) – precludes any referentiality to a context outside the poem, let alone to the representation of cultural identity. His nostalgia for the heroic times of naturalism, a discourse presumably elaborated through an exacting economy of meaning, and his call for an aesthetics founded on rationality privilege narrative and its ability to communicate ideas cogently. For Rodó, the cognitive logic of narrative is the principal factor that allows his essays to propagandize and even be considered manifestos for a Spanish American identity. In his essay on Darío's poetics, he writes: "toda manifestación de poesía ha sido más o menos subyugada en América por la suprema necesidad de la propaganda y la acción. El arte no ha sido, por lo general, sino la forma más remontada de la propaganda; y poesía que lucha no puede ser poesía que cincela" [every manifestation of poetry has been more or less subjugated in America by the supreme necessity of propaganda and action. Art has not been, in general, but the earliest form of propaganda; and poetry that struggles cannot be poetry that chisels] (*Obras completas*, p. 170). These denunciations originate not abroad but in the prose of a fellow Spanish American writer. The struggle between Rodó and Darío to champion their respective ideals of a pan-Hispanic voice cannot be exclusively determined by a Spanish/Spanish American juxtaposition.

Yet these first assessments of the *modernista* literary expression fueled subsequent contentions over the geocultural borders between Spanish and Spanish American literatures. As Sharman concisely states, literary history "funciona a manera de guardia, patrullando las fronteras de la cultura, anunciando diferencias tajantes, conjurando los 'elementos extranjeros' que amenazan con hender el nombre propio" [functions in the manner of a guard, patrolling culture's frontiers, announcing categorical differences, warding off the "foreign elements" that threaten to split apart the name itself] (p. 333). Three articles in Lily Litvak's compilation of critical essays, *El modernismo*, exemplify Sharman's observation by clearly illustrating how the movement and its literary criticism provided a discourse about national patrimonies.[4] In other criticism from the same period, Gordon Brotherston summarizes a major disagreement over the movement's literary and national lineage when he claims that there was an unstated though tangible opposition between what he calls the Peninsular and the Hispano-American approaches to *modernismo* ("La poesía andaluza y modernista de Manuel Machado," p. 267). In making this observation, Brotherston successfully exposes the nationalistic polarized stances between which literary critics of *modernismo* tend to position their arguments. For the most part, he identifies the Peninsular camp with the completeness of a Spanish national literature and the Americanists with the commerce of transnational intertextualities. Bernardo Gicovate suggests that the difference between the Peninsular and the Hispano-American critiques of the movement corresponds to a moment of a historical attitude. He points out that the Spanish writer, with the exception of Valle-Inclán's *Tirano Banderas*, is interested in the Hispanoamerican literary production only "fraternalmente" [fraternally], whereas the Hispano-American writer has always considered Spanish patrimony as his or her bona fide heritage ("Antes del modernismo," p. 199). Ivan A. Shulman perceives the antithesis differently. He postulates that the disparity between the literary expressions on both sides of the Atlantic is reducible to the ephemeral character of Peninsular *modernismo,* which is a condition that differs from the persistence of its American counterpart ("Reflexiones en torno a la definición del modernismo," p. 354).

The main contention of those critics who support the immutable continuity of Spanish literature is that *modernismo* was a temporary divergence from an authentic Spanish literary expression. And Pedro Salinas is perhaps the most provocative of this group. In his article "El problema del modernismo en España, o un conflicto entre dos espíritus," he develops a theory about the difference between the generation of 1898 and the *modernistas* that is based on distinctions between the supposed cosmopolitanism and syntheticism of the latter and the introspection and intellectualism of the former (pp. 24–5). When he turns his attention to Juan Ramón Jiménez's *modernista* poetry and, in particular, to *Eternidades,* Salinas characterizes Jiménez's poems as examples of an innocence that subsequently changed into a "cansancio y disgusto por ese concepto de la poesía" [weariness and distaste for that concept of poetry] (p. 31). For Salinas, Jiménez's transcendence of the *modernista* aesthetics typifies a generation of Spanish poets. He reasserts the primacy of Spanish poetry by claiming that the *modernista* "deviance" still remains within the borders of a Spanish literary tradition (p. 34).

What Salinas criticizes in *modernismo* is not just the digression of its proponents from a literary canon but the seemingly arbitrary manner by which the movement's members take apart and reassemble the landmarks and boundaries of their literary tradition in order to privilege, according to him, a beautiful and seductive language for its own sake. Salinas and others generally associate this poetic practice with the hegemony that French Symbolism and Parnassianism enjoyed at the turn of the century. Schulman argues that the *modernistas* were inclined to "desplazar lo español y entronizar lo francés" [displace Spanishness and enthrone Frenchness] ("Reflexiones en torno a la definición del modernismo," p. 350). As far as this infiltration of French cultural referents is concerned, John W. Kronik considers it impossible to deny the impact of French literary movements on *modernismo,* and

that those who do so "han sufrido sin duda un descaminado patri-
otismo cultural, si no un toque de xenofobia" [have undoubtedly
suffered a wayward cultural patriotism, if not a touch of xeno-
phobia] (p. 39). These metaphors of veering off the road capture
the posture that writers and critics have taken as they ascertain and
even attempt to counteract perceived threats to the coherence of
national literatures and cultural identities. In the final analysis, it is
these critical efforts to disparage the *modernistas'* disassembly of
European cultural artifacts that inadvertently attest to the centrality of the movement's cultural work in Spanish American societies. Needless to say, the dangers that apparently menace this
coherence cannot be fully evaluated without exploring the political economy of the Spanish American objectification and assimilation of foreign literatures.

Although the critics who defend the integrity of Spanish literature disapprove of divergences from canonized models and affini-
ties toward external influences, those who promote *modernista* aesthetics champion the same errancy in the name not only of an
artistic but also of a cultural freedom of expression. On this side of
the debate, a figurative language of commercial interests informs
national and regional agendas and provides a consistent subtext.
José Martí promotes the freedom of autonomous expression by
contesting why non-Spanish literatures should be considered forbidden fruit ("Oscar Wilde," p. 60). After illustrating the influence
of other European literatures in the works of Spanish poets, Martí
concludes: "Conocer diversas literaturas es el medio mejor de lib-
ertarse de la tiranía de algunas de ellas" [Knowing diverse literatures is the best means of liberating oneself from the tyranny of
some of them] (p. 60). What Martí proposes is the broadening of
the horizon to an influx of literatures from a variety of sources. By
liberalizing the trade in cultural contributions to Spanish American cultural autonomy, Martí undermines the Spanish monopoly
of that commerce. Ramos notes that it was because of his "voluntad
de autonomía de lo político [que] Martí veía positivamente la
emergencia de un mercado literario, separado de las instituciones
del Estado" [desire for autonomy from the political [that] Martí
saw the emergence of a literary market, separated from State insti-

tutions, in positive terms] (p. 72). This separation from state institutions was crucial for the Cuban poet and journalist because,
unlike that of other *modernistas* in independent Spanish American
countries, Martí's cultural agenda for Cuba under Spanish rule was
radically anticolonial.

By continuing to insist that Spanish American literature is characterized by an openness to the outside world, Octavio Paz ampli-
fies Martí's appeal for greater intertextual commerce. However, it
is worth noting that in this amplification, Paz's critical inquiry slips
into a dispute between national and regional identities:

La crítica tampoco ha podido explicarnos enteramente por qué el
movimiento modernista, que se inicia como una adaptación de la
poesía francesa en nuestra lengua, comienza antes en Hispanoamérica que en España. Cierto, los hispanoamericanos hemos sido
y somos más sensibles a lo que pasa en el mundo que los españoles,
menos prisioneros de nuestra tradición y nuestra historia. ("Traducción y metáfora," p. 106)

[Nor has criticism been able to explain to us completely why the *modernista* movement, which starts out as an adaptation of French poetry
in our language, begins earlier in Hispano-America than in Spain.
Certainly, we Hispano-Americans have been and are more sensitive to
what goes on in the world than Spaniards, less imprisoned by our tradition and our history.]

Paz responds to a literary question by invoking a cultural determinism. He reinforces this invocation by assuming that Spaniards
are more tradition-bound and less likely to embrace cultural differences than Hispano-Americans. Offering proof of the Spanish
American spirit of openness and intellectual free trade at the turn
of the century, he writes in the same study: "En esos años las clases
dirigentes y los grupos intelectuales de América Latina descubren
la filosofía positivista y la abrazan con entusiasmo. Cambiamos las
máscaras de Danton y Jefferson por las de Auguste Comte y Herbert
Spencer" [In those years Latin America's ruling classes and intellectual groups discover positivist philosophy and embrace it enthusiastically. We exchanged the masks of Danton and Jefferson for
those of Auguste Comte and Herbert Spencer] (p. 104). For the

Mexican poet, the Hispano-American position is candid and self-critical; it is capable of adjusting itself to the intellectual currents of precise historical moments. Paz's choice of the metaphor "máscara" [mask] implies that the Spanish American intellectual can incorporate, objectify, and employ philosophical and political systems at will. This openness and the autonomy that it subsequently provides, however, rely on an active trade or exchange of intellectual postures. This argument is diametrically opposed to Salinas' transformation of Spanish literary traditions into cultural icons. In his depiction of Spanish Americans as less dependent on their traditions than Spaniards are on theirs, Paz's metaphor of incarceration represents the antithesis of the freedom to abandon the road in order to participate in transnational intellectual commerce.

Beginning in the 1960s, sociological interpretations of the movement countered the argument that the *modernistas* eluded their societies by illustrating that their works were the products of particular socioeconomic circumstances. Renewed interest in *modernismo* in 1967, the centenary of Darío's birth, included attempts to provide the movement's members with greater social relevance. That year, a more socioeconomic strain of criticism began with the publication of Angel Rama's *Los poetas modernistas en el mercado económico* and continued in Françoise Pérus, *Literatura y sociedad en América Latina: el modernismo* (1975); in a number of articles in Lily Litvak's critical anthology *El modernismo* (1975); and in Noé Jitrik, *Las contradicciones del modernismo* (1978). These studies and others distinguished the *modernistas* as artists whose works registered the difficult transition from patronage to professionalization in the modern production of literature. Because valuable attention was being paid to the movement's writing as a skilled craft, critical focus shifted toward examining how poets and writers perceived their societal role in manifestos, prologues, essays on aesthetics, modernity, and national and regional politics. Critics became especially interested in the journalism of figures like José Martí, Rubén Darío, and Manuel Gutiérrez Nájera.[5] Although these approaches to Spanish American *modernismo* have multiplied and differ in the degree of agency that they ascribe to the movement's members, all invariably attest to the centrality of the *modernista* artist in the production of culture.

This centrality of the *modernistas* in the production of culture is often associated with economic expansion, especially in the more vulgar Marxist readings. As I have already argued, the emergence of bourgeois capitalism informs the kind of language in which the *modernistas* imagined and expressed Spanish America's cultural autonomy. However, those interpretations that overemphasize economic growth by failing to interrogate the *modernistas'* ambivalent feelings toward the political economy of their literary production risk depoliticizing the poets' and writers' rhetorical stances by subsuming them under quantitative criteria such as the progression of the movement in direct proportion to the physical extension of its readership. In *Imagined Communities* (1983), Benedict Anderson illustrates that economic development and its concomitant extension of print technology are important factors that facilitated the imagined idea of the nation. But these factors cannot account entirely for the selective appeals that *modernistas* made as they created and cultivated very specific reading constituencies; they do not fully illuminate the foundation of a cultural literacy. We should move beyond the assumption that once they are disseminated by print technology, political messages are equally accessible or palatable to all readers within the reach of scribal culture. Readers are discerning subjects who are capable of modulating their responses to texts, reading with or against their communicated meanings. In short, the press is not a necessarily hegemonic manipulator of thoughts. One of my intentions in this study is to depart from this model of absolute determinism by an infrastructure and to posit the *modernista* politics of identity as a process that takes place through cultivated aesthetic experiences.

By exquisite design

To claim that the *modernistas* refused to involve themselves in the cultural politics of their times is a way avoiding areas of inquiry that are crucial for the way we speak not only about the *modernista* canon but also about our positions as literary critics who continue the cultural criticism that the *modernistas* began over a hundred years ago. When Néstor García Canclini accounts for the gap between a "modernismo exuberante" [exuberant modernism] and a "modernización deficiente" [deficient modernization] ("Contradicciones latinoamericanas," p. 371), he rightly points to the powerful role of economic and intellectual elites who "*se hacen cargo de la intersección de diferentes temporalidades históricas y tratan de elaborar con ellas un proyecto global*" [*take charge of the intersection of different historical temporalities and try to produce a global project with them*] (p. 376). Today's criticism enjoys more secure accommodations in universities, publishing houses, and the press than the uncertain institutional and commercial housing that the *modernistas'* work occupied at the turn of the century. Yet it is precisely because of the continuities that link their cultural work and ours that it would be illuminating to examine how and when these institutions and enterprises made it possible for critics to assume and claim a "professional objectivity."

Although such valuable historical work is beyond the scope of my current investigation, I am prepared to postulate that in such a study revealing connections could probably be found between the *modernistas'* detachment and the "objectivity" of contemporary critics. How coincidental can it be, for example, that their aloofness and our "objectivity" correspond to similar notions of power exercised from outside and above that I mentioned earlier as forms of engagement? Most instructive in a project of that sort would be an analysis of the degree to which the conventional insistence on the *modernistas'* detachment has inadvertently ended up expressing and recording an anxiety of influence on the part of literary critics. It could be that this kind of accusation against the movement's members has conveniently served over the years to camouflage the tangible influence of critics by reinforcing the notion that they wield insignificant authority or that their work is nominally political in comparison with that of statesmen, politicians, technocrats, and the like. However, as I noted regarding Valle-Castillo's and Olivencia's comments, the ability to invoke, name, and qualify nationalism and pan-Hispanism through language and, furthermore, the wherewithal to carry out these functions in the public sphere, greatly influence the terms that are used to signify and thereby coordinate the agenda for these debates.

By illustrating the connections between the *modernistas'* work and that of today's critics, it becomes possible to visualize worthwhile fields of comparative investigation and hence propose new hypotheses. For instance, there are uncanny parallels between the promises that economic liberalism held for Spanish America at the turn of the century and the "globalization" of economic markets and culture – the new cosmopolitanism – that the North American Free Trade Agreement works toward building throughout the Americas as we enter a new century. Some of the issues being rehearsed once more include: arguments for the liberalization of the continent's markets; agreements for economic union and cultural exchange; discussions about the feasibility of various regional configurations, especially since the push toward creating unified markets profoundly affects political models of national sovereignty; and the debate over the United States' ability to promote its definition of modernity beyond its borders. These discussions provide fresh opportunities for conceptualizing the significance of closer economic and cultural ties throughout the Americas and, therefore, attest to the striking resemblance between this *fin de siècle* and the last. Whereas late nineteenth-century statesmen and their spokesmen heralded the rise and the benefits of expanding free markets, their twentieth-century counterparts advertise the promise of a post-Cold War order. Both periods ought to be examined with an eye toward interrogating both this rhetoric of a new dawn and the advocates of that uncomplicated prophecy.[6]

Because of the nature of this intellectual and cultural work, literary critics are unavoidably engaged in the discursive construction of identities. Therefore, it is essential, as Schulman has recently argued, to study not just the origins of *modernismo* but those of its criticism as well ("Hacia un discurso crítico del modernismo concebido como sistema," p. 267). Analogous to the way in which Rodó simultaneously attacked *modernismo* for its views on Americanism and modernity and reminisced about the virtues of naturalism, today's critics privilege or devalue certain discourses, question or promote the formation and relevance of literary canons and other icons of literacy, and, in short, help to determine the languages that express cultural locations. Like the *modernistas*, critics continue to create meaning by reformulating literary commonplaces and breathing new life into tropes.[7] Certainly, part of the critic's task is to imagine the historical moment of a text's prior readership. But this task is not the same as the uncritical attempt to reconstruct an entire historical period – as if so absolute a restoration were indeed possible. Hence, as I look back at the movement, I recognize that my approaches to it are in varying degrees unavoidably modulated by current, critical concerns. In this study, I have employed contemporary, interpretive readings to reveal how the *modernistas* constructed class, transnational, and racial alliances for and with their reading constituencies. The admission that this project is contemporary yet historical to the extent that it offers insights into Spanish America's literary production toward the end of the last century permits me to highlight the principal activity that we literary critics have in common with the *modernistas*: the intellectual and cultural work of assessing and determining literacies. In order to examine their involvement in this work, let us now turn to a definition of the ways in which the *modernistas* sought to engage their readers.

The *modernistas* anticipated and attempted to establish an exclusive dialogue among their ranks and with specific readers *by exquisite design*. In coining this phrase, I mean to emphasize and interrogate the combined artistry and purposefulness of the movement's literature. I use the word "design" not only to refer to an aesthetic practice embedded in local and transnational cultural politics and institutions but also to show how this self-conscious practice cannot be separated from the *modernistas*' preoccupation with and involvement in their uncertain profession(alism). The term, therefore, signals the complementariness of the movement's aesthetics and cultural politics. These artists and intellectuals cultivated their exquisite literary style precisely to generate a particular reciprocity with their reading public. In exchange for successfully negotiated social and professional positions, they provided Spanish American ruling classes with works containing and promoting utopian alliances that served to affirm or transcend national boundaries. To elucidate this negotiated exchange, my study consistently focuses on two areas of cultural and political activity in every chapter: the first area describes and examines the degree to which *modernista* aesthetics created and promoted distinctions between competent or at least appreciative readers and "less privileged" – that is, the unenlightened and/or dissenting ones. This discrimination on the basis of cultural literacy, exemplifying an early version of what Arjun Appadurai recently called "the imagination as a social practice" (p. 5), constitutes to a great extent the discursive work of making culture.[8] The second area illustrates some of the ways in which the *modernistas* were responsible for initiating those aesthetic and professional practices that have given rise to particular forums for literary criticism in Spanish America today.

Viewing the imagination as a site of conflict requires a reader-response approach to texts that also addresses the social antagonisms contained in them. With respect to the possibilities of determining the reading audience, Wolfgang Iser and Hans Robert Jauss offer useful insights. For Iser, "literary texts initiate 'performances' of meaning" (pp. 26–7) in which "iconic signs of literature . . . designate *instructions* for the *production* of the signified" (p. 65). Jauss postulates that "the horizon of expectations of a work allows one to determine its artistic character by the kind and degree of its influence on a presumed audience" (p. 25). Both critics describe reading as an aesthetic experience through which one can perceive the writer's agency not just as the producer of a text but also as an act of mutual recognition or interpellation between the writer and the reading public. Here lies the power of their phenomenology of self and collective identity. However, by confining this experience to the institutional boundaries of literary history, these critics limit their conceptualization of the writer's agency. Iser's "implied reader" is meant to "allow for the reader's presence without in any way determining his character or his historical situation" (p. 34), and Jauss's "horizon of expectations" is accessible as a "literary experience of contemporary and later readers, critics, and authors" (p. 22). In both cases, the literary imagination is not a locus of political activism.

With respect to the social context of reading, and especially to the reading of poetry for the ways in which it can appeal to its audience or readers through ideology, I have found Ron Silliman's ideas germane to my critical approach. "The primary ideological message of poetry," Silliman states,

> lies not in its explicit content, political though that may be, but in the attitude toward reception it demands of the reader. It is this "attitude towards information" which is carried forward by the recipient. It is this attitude which forms the basis for a response to other information, not necessarily literary, in the text. And, beyond the poem, in the world. (p. 31)

The inculcation of this "attitude towards information" clearly describes the role of the pre-texts and, specifically, of the prologues and opening editorial remarks that I examine in this study. But in addition to considering these prefaces as necessary introductions to *modernista* aesthetics, my objective has also been to show how certain poetic texts might have been evaluated in their time. In his essay on the political economy of poetry, Silliman begins to determine the theoretical configurations of such critical assessments: "Context determines (and is determined by) both the motives of the readers and their experience, their history, i.e., their literary product, without which communication of a message (formal, substantive, ideological) cannot occur" (p. 25). Likewise, in her attempt to investigate the potential for a Marxist aesthetics, Michèle Barrett argues that "meaning is not immanent; it is constructed in the consumption of the work. Hence, no text can be inherently progressive or reactionary; it becomes so in the act of consumption" (p. 702). Barrett's argument can be appreciated, but in interrogating the social circumstances of a particular readership, it is essential to supplement her notion of meaning through consumption with Silliman's view that context is also determined by experience and history.

The kind of reader reception in which I am interested partly

relies on Louis Althusser's definition of writing and reading as "rit-
uals of ideological recognition" ("Ideology and Ideological State
Apparatuses," p. 173). In another significant text, "Preface to
Capital Volume One," he explains this definition further by illustrating that basically two sorts of readers confront the abstractions
in Marx's work: those who experience capitalist exploitation (pro-
letarian and nonproletarian wage laborers) and those who are
ruled by bourgeois ideology. Althusser perceives these confrontations as a class struggle that ensues at the level of the text's interpretation and subsequent utility. He presents his guide to reading
Capital not as "mere *education*" but as a route toward "a real *rupture*"
and revolutionary consciousness (p. 10). These observations about
an ideologically sustained reading process are well reasoned and
useful, but they also betray a place and historical moment that are
different from the focus of this study. Althusser was interested in
critiquing bourgeois culture in a way that advocated a complete –
and with hindsight, impossible – break with capitalism in modern
metropolitan centers. As I have already noted, the politics of
Spanish American *modernismo* takes place in a period in which the
movement's members and readers were seeking to join and even
compete with those metropolitan centers from the periphery.
Cosmopolitanism was the discourse that they used to differentiate
themselves from former colonial powers only insofar as that differentiation gave them access to an equal status, to a prestige that was
on par with that of former colonizers. Nevertheless, what I would
like to retain from Althusser is the notion that certain "abstractions" (in this study, the cultivated exquisiteness and, hence, exclusivity of *modernista* aesthetics) can be intentionally employed in the
processes of writing and reading to draw and withdraw, for
example, the borders between particular classes and nations.

  In addition to a method of reading for discriminating strategies
and abstractions, what is needed in order to comprehend the *modernistas'* ability to exercise power from outside and above is a
theory of manipulative ideology that does not dismiss their location in high culture. As a purveyor of ruling-class ideology, in other
words, how can *modernista* aesthetics be considered politically

expedient? Fredric Jameson envisions such a scenario when he argues in *The Political Unconscious* (1981) that

> the achieved collectivity or organic group of whatever kind – oppressors fully as much as oppressed – is Utopian not in itself, but only insofar as all such collectivities are themselves *figures* for the ultimate concrete collective life of an achieved Utopian or classless society. Now we are in a better position to understand how even hegemonic or ruling-class culture and ideology are Utopian, not in spite of their instrumental function to secure and perpetuate class privilege and power, but rather precisely because that function is also in and of itself the affirmation of collective solidarity. (p. 291)

Jameson's view of the dialectical relationship between ideology and utopia is distinguishable from Althusser's notion of the same relationship in "Ideology and Ideological State Apparatuses" by its greater emphasis on the rallying power of the collectivity's representations or "figures" rather than on the established collectivity itself. Recruiting this emphasis on the potential for artistic mediators to convey a utopian, communal meaning allows me to point out how the *modernistas* and their public created and promoted a particular social imaginary by determining and refining the rules of a class-based, cultural literacy.

From, on the one hand, the notion that literary texts are the private reserve of its author to the widest dissemination of these texts through the press on the other, the chapters in this book describe forms of critical/political engagement that gradually extend their horizons of influence. In Chapter 2, I examine some of Darío's prologues. These metatexts outline the kinds of social relevance and intellectual attachments that, in negating, the poet paradoxically reaffirmed. Concentrating on the language of these texts, I investigate the source of the claim that the *modernistas* were detached: Darío's (and others') famous *reino interior* [interior realm]. This internal realm or space has been characterized as the site of the *modernista* interiority, the ivory tower of the movement's members, the place of their hermetic literary production. I have posited this space as a consciously invoked though ironic locus of literary production because it exemplifies an ambiguous resistance to the marketplace. Darío cultivated this ambiguity to his advantage, and the success of this strategic ambiguity may be seen in his refusal to allow his art to serve as a model for a movement that he simultaneously professed to lead. The egocentric focus of Darío's poetics is not surprising once we consider that he wrote his poetry and prose within a tradition that Michael Holquist has called the "personalist" way of understanding language: "I own meaning" (pp. 163–4). According to this conception of language, any representation of exteriority will be founded on that proprietorship of meaning.

In addition to being a conceptual site of literary production, the *reino interior* also became a critical register that facilitated the discussion of a variety of cultural issues and agendas. It is worth underscoring the ultimately dialogical character of this realm. The *reino interior* signifies beyond its representations of internal spaces to say something about the social circumstances that gave rise to its literary creation and refinement in *modernista* texts. Toward the development of this analysis, I also examine in this chapter a series of critical articles on Julián del Casal's work that were published right after his death. That poet's contemporaries and subsequent critics evaluated his literary production in ways that contributed to the foundation of a psychosocial approach to interpreting literature at the turn of the century.

Because *modernismo* is noted for its abundant poetry as well as for its expression of Spanish American cultural independence from Spanish literary traditions, the movement ought to be explored with a view toward elucidating this connection between poetry and the construction of identity. This task is one that I undertake in Chapter 3. The infrequency of such an exercise may be due to a prejudice that rejects the lyrical – because of a perceived, generic propensity toward a language that is exquisite and thus distracting – in favor of prose's supposed ability to transmit direct, objective meanings. Suffice it to say for the moment that there is a record of efforts among critics to champion one genre over the other (see Castillo, p. 9). Enrique Anderson-Imbert, however, characterizes "Salutación del optimista" and other poems from Darío's *Cantos de vida y esperanza* as representative of the poet's return to social concerns ("Los poemas cívicos de 1905," p. 172). The importance of

"Salutación del optimista" lies in the textual and contextual circumstances of its inaugural performance before an eminent audience of literary connoisseurs at the Ateneo de Madrid in 1905. Although the momentous contingency of those circumstances has transpired, the poem's performance conserves a residual presence in the text.

With respect to the process of engaging his readers in order to promote a specific view of Spanish America, José Enrique Rodó's essay *Ariel* differs ostensibly from Darío's advocacy of a *reino interior*. Most of the criticism on the essay has canonized the work as the epitome of a Hispano-American autonomous expression at the turn of the century. This canonization is based on the view that the essay is an elegantly argued outcry against North American cultural hegemony and imperialism. Published two years after the Spanish American War in which Spain lost its last overseas possessions, *Ariel* – as Gordon Brotherston remarks in his edition – had to be read as a manifesto. If *Ariel* clearly defines Spanish Americanism, then the language in which this autonomy is described should be illuminating. With this concern in mind, I examine specific aspects of the essay's intertextuality. Rodó's text is ambiguously *modernista*; its style has much in common with some of Darío's writings. Also, few critics have looked at the manner in which Rodó appropriated other discourses in order to give his essay originality and the authority to become an icon of resistance to North American culture. By observing the kinds of concepts that Rodó discards and retains at different stages in the essay, I will be heeding Jean Franco's insistence that critics should begin to examine those acts of borrowing more closely.[9]

The dialogue that Rodó established with the intellectual traditions of his time was also facilitated by a political economy of literary production, a critical practice, in which the Uruguayan circulated his work. *Ariel* has been made into a cultural icon, fetishized to the degree that it is almost impossible to distinguish in its criticism the essay (*Ariel*) from the statue (Ariel). This confusion worked to Rodó's benefit from the start. At the turn of the century, authors relied on an elaborate and influential network of correspondence among writers, poets, literary critics, politicians, and the like. In Rodó's letters to his literary friends and even to critics he did not know, he clearly worked toward raising *Ariel* to the heights of a cultural flag.

In Chapter 5, I turn my attention to some of the *modernista* literary reviews that gave the idea of transnational Hispanism tangible representation. These periodicals were important writing spaces for disseminating national and transnational identities. Although the contingency of journalism and nationalism is historically verifiable, writing in periodicals and its technical support and facilities are not the cause of patriotic sentiment. Benedict Anderson entertains this hypothesis by theorizing what he refers to as print languages and the manner in which these work through a homogeneous and instantaneous reading process to foster a national consciousness. This conception of the connections between language, writing, reading, and consciousness needs further complication. It owes much of its emphasis on the technical to an insistence on an immediacy of consciousness that a particular technology facilitates. At worst, this reliance on Walter Benjamin's notion of "aura" results in damaging and prejudicial statements against Spanish American national experiences.[10] Consequently, I have devoted a good portion of the chapter to examining Anderson's views. What his notion of an instantaneous, national consciousness does not explain is the complex desire for national and regional communities. This desire finds some of its most overt manifestations in the editorial goals of *modernista* reviews. In the opening numbers of the reviews, the editors describe the kinds of literature that they promise to offer their readers and at the same time not only concern themselves with explicating and advocating their aesthetic guidelines but reinforce these endeavors by promoting national and regional sentiments.

In the concluding chapter, I examine and theorize the *modernistas*' importation of literary and cultural artifacts from metropolitan centers in order to summarize this study and also propose future areas of worthwhile investigation. I associate these areas with consumption. For whether or not it was true that the *modernistas* were solely interested in promoting an art for its own sake (this argument is itself an appropriation of "European theories" about modern art), this accusation can be contextualized as a pan-Hispanic debate about economic liberalism and the creation of a language of cultural identity. As I have shown, the movement's poetics were described as a deviance from the genealogical continuity of Spanish literary traditions, as the perverse enjoyment of materialism, and at the same time as an incipient awareness of a pan-Hispanic identity. Although these nineteenth-century discourses on race (*raza*), class, and transnationalism are identifiable in *modernista* poetics and its criticism, they have been characterized for the most part in negative terms. In this final chapter, I offer an alternative view of these "negative" or supposedly overdetermined aspects. For it is by interrogating the nature of the *modernista*'s so-called excesses and detachment that it becomes possible to situate and critique their status and politics in Spanish American societies at the end of the nineteenth century.

2

The *reino interior*

Any attempt to demonstrate the *modernistas'* influence in their societies must first address the movement's most frequently identified trope: the *reino interior*. In order to challenge the claim that the *modernistas* sought asylum in sublime interior spaces removed from the demands of political and economic life and expressed that desire for an escapist contemplation in their literature, it is essential to examine the contours of this private area of introspection, imagination, and literary production. Darío, for example, promoted this realm as the unique source of his talent, influence, and fame. With its thick walls and tranquil inner recesses, the architecture of this figurative space lends itself to the conception of a subjectivity that is either besieged or geared for an offensive. These bellicose postures are scarcely the kind that one would associate with a group of presumably self-absorbed aesthetes; but for those who subscribe to the evasive detachment hypothesis, it is the walls of this *reino interior* that by definition resist or confront the social. In this chapter, I examine some of Darío's most famous statements concerning both his aesthetics and literary production in Spanish America at the turn of the century. In purporting to write literature within a nonsocial space, not only did this poet attempt to create a unique professional sphere for himself but, in so doing, he provided his bourgeois and well-to-do readers with a social imaginary grounded in class exclusivity. That the *reino interior* should merge professional concerns with this imaginary is hardly coincidental. Such a combination illustrates the kind of engagement that Darío sought from his reading constituencies. My focus on Darío is intentional. Although he may not be the first *modernista*, he is certainly the movement's most visible figure and, among his writings, his prologues and essays on aesthetics clearly reveal that he and other *modernistas* possessed elaborate ideas about their instrumental role in Spanish American societies and culture.

As a literary commonplace, the *reino interior* descends from the Western tradition of the *locus amoenus* – or the site, roughly, where nature and the writing subject's self-awareness are mutually and inextricably constituted through a symbolic language. The *modernistas'* innovation and tendency, however, was to situate their contemplation indoors. In their literature, there are abundant descriptions of salons, drawing-rooms, cells in castles and monasteries, alcoves, medieval or preindustrial work-rooms, and other private niches. It is from and through these real and imagined spaces that Manuel Gutiérrez Nájera and Julián del Casal, for instance, draw their inspiration to create sublime realms in which the mundane is either deemed extraneous or invoked in a disparaging fashion. This celebration of privacy does not merely represent a reprieve from the burdensome uncertainties and demands of economic life; the *modernistas'* idealization of these exclusive sanctuaries also emblematized and hence captured the aspirations of the monied classes to cultivate the art of leisure away from the "debasing" commercial and industrial labor upon which they depended for their own economic welfare. A good example of these bids may be found in one of the foremost *modernista* reviews. In the opening editorial remarks of the *Revista Azul*'s first issue (1894), Gutiérrez Nájera describes the publication as a special house and promises his readers that he would stand at the bottom of the stairs in order to prevent the unworthy – that is, the uncultivated, the envious, and the plebeian – from ascending and entering the fine salons upstairs (p. 2). Conversely, and in a familiar representation of incompatibilities between the interior and exterior, it is no surprise that when the poet and protagonist in Darío's famous story "El rey burgués" is abandoned outdoors, he finds himself exiled from any site of spiritual repose and eventually dies, after having been nonchalantly relegated by the bourgeois king to the status of a collectible.

What also interests me about this imaginary is not only that the celebration of privacy and the production of literature coincide in the *reino interior* but the subsequent transformation of this figurative space into a critical commonplace. In addition to being a site that was described using a *fin de siècle* psychoanalytic language – for the most part, an approach to *modernista* texts that identified them with the "pathological" or at least deviant behavior of their authors – this realm has constituted a field of social discourse about the relationship between aesthetics and (trans)national cultures. To substantiate this hypothesis, I elucidate the case of Julián del Casal when his famous contemporaries commented on the poet's works and life shortly after his death. Most of their discussions centered on determining the constitution and boundaries of his ego. In most of these critical pieces, there is overwhelming agreement about a certain aspect of Casal's character and the ways that it influenced his literary production: the poet was, as one of his biographers puts it, "la más angustiada figura" [the most anguished figure] of Cuban literary history (Armas, p. 29). According to his critics, Casal had been imprisoned in a time and place that proved too adverse for his refined sensibilities and idealism; he epitomized the artist besieged by the professionalization of his vocation and concomitantly troubled by the knowledge that he had lost his social prestige in spite of his supposedly esteemed finesse. Casal's situation interests me because his penury forced him to live in a room behind the office of *La Habana Elegante*, the review he edited. Within these quarters, the *reino interior* apparently assumed an existential condition.

A modernista *site of literary production*

In "Poetry and Politics," Hans Magnus Enzensberger elucidates the relationship that existed between political power and poetry by tracing the history of the literary convention known as the eulogy. The tradition of patronizing the arts evolved out of a need to translate a reign's material prestige into the posterity of a favorably recorded history. In form and content, the eulogy immortalized its subject – the patron as epic hero – by means of a particular economic mode of literary production (patronage). Yet by the time the *modernistas* were espousing their aesthetics, it had become evident that the promotion of the patron as an epic subject of history was being outpaced by novel forms of patronage and collective self-praise. Noting the simultaneity of traditional and new forms of support for the arts around the time of *Azul*'s publication, Diana Sorensen Goodrich points out that it had been the custom to have wealthy friends finance a first edition. This practice continued at the same time that the developing bourgeoisie, with its solid income and leisure time, preferred buying and reading newspapers (p. 6). Referring to these new clients and the demands that they made on the production of literature, Walter Benjamin writes:

The crowd – no subject was more entitled to the attention of the nineteenth-century writers. It was getting ready to take shape as a public in broad strata who had acquired facility in reading. It became a customer; it wished to find itself portrayed in the contemporary novel, as patrons did in the paintings of the Middle Ages. (*Charles Baudelaire: A Lyric Poet in the Era of High Capitalism*, p. 120)

Hence, other conventions began to address the complex relationship that these new customers maintained with their spokesmen and their preferred modes of self-representation; but because they are relegated to a space outside the literary text, these conventions are often taken as the benign and almost decorative formalities of the writing industry. Many of them, such as forewords, dedicatories, acknowledgments, and prologues, deserve more meticulous scrutiny because they rhetorically engage the historical, economic, and institutional circumstances in which they, and the texts they precede, were written. Furthermore, they describe how and where these texts and their authors posit themselves, that is, establish their difference and originality in various fields of social activity.

The pretextual space has often been chosen by writers or read by literary critics as a locus for the agendas of literary movements. Such is the case with the prologues to three of Rubén Darío's books of poetry and prose: "Palabras liminares," from *Prosas profanas* (1896); the unnamed prologue to *Cantos de vida y esperanza* (1905); and "Dilucidaciones," from *El canto errante* (1907).[1] In these texts, Darío makes direct references to his aesthetics and its reception by hostile critics, and it is for that reason that the texts were subsequently regarded as programmatic documents, as personal declarations of a *modernista ars poetica*. Nevertheless, because Darío unabashedly claimed personal responsibility for the successful renovation of Spanish lyrical forms, it is not surprising that his declarations were aggrandized to the status of manifestos that had plotted the movement's direction. Since the literary work, from its intellectual conception to its physical appearance in the market, is a collective endeavor, one may easily dismiss Darío's view as egocentric, as a gross misrepresentation of the circumstances surrounding the production of literature. However, this "misrepresentation" should not be disregarded. That Darío envisions the success of a literary movement as his personal handicraft already posits a social statement – specifically, one that involves him in polemics concerning the production of art in that society. One cannot appreciate the importance of Darío's attitude by proving whether or not the exclusion of the social in the production of literature and culture is possible but, instead, by revealing how Darío imagines the social to be irrelevant.

In "Palabras liminares," Darío declares that he is in full possession of his art: "Mi literatura es *mía* en mí" [My literature is mine in me] (p. 8). The importance of this statement, especially since the poet deems it necessary to explain and insist upon the correct meaning of these words in two subsequent prologues, cannot be overlooked. In the declaration, one which Noé Jitrik refers to as an "afirmación de mismidad" [an affirmation of selfness] (p. 6), the containment of literature is almost absolute. Not only is the possessive adjective ("mi") reinforced by the pronoun that follows ("*mía*"), but the copulative structure is also absorbed and sealed within ("en mí"). Darío locates the production of literature within himself, and, in the prologue to *Cantos de vida y esperanza*, he even interprets this hermetic conception of literature as an essential part of his life. He explains: "Cuando dije que mi poesía era 'mía, en mí' sostuve la primera condición de mi existir, sin pretensión alguna de causar sectarismo en mente o voluntad ajena, y en un íntimo amor a lo absoluto de la belleza" [When I said that my poetry was "mine, in me" I sustained the first condition of my existence without any claim toward causing sectarianism in the minds and will of others and in an intimate love for the absoluteness of beauty] (p. 11). He attenuates the apologetic tone of the explanation by broadening the importance of the interior space of literary production in "Palabras liminares" to represent in the other prologues an existential condition ("la primera condición de mi existir"). Not only does Darío link literary production in this manner to his reason for being but he also associates this singleness of purpose with the sacred: "Al seguir la vida que Dios me ha concedido tener, he buscado expresarme lo más noble y altamente en mi comprensión" [In following the life that God has allowed me to have, I have sought to express myself as nobly and loftily as I know how] (*Cantos de vida y esperanza*, p. 11). A fundamental issue in this stance resides in Darío's allusions to the sacred. Why should Darío have recourse to the sacred at the same time that he is advocating the self-sufficiency of his art? Literally, this respect for God allows Darío to imply that his artistic expression has been conceded by divine right; figuratively, it suggests that his work ought to be considered pure and complete – that is to say, incomparable. In both cases, the poet is arguing for a conception of literary production that sanctifies the book and transforms it into a uniquely attractive object of acquisition.

When he imagines and advocates the "sacred" integrity of his books, what Darío accomplishes is the creation of a formidable effect in which the book comes to represent the objectification of his creativity. As such, his genius can be appreciated as an object *in its totality*. In "The Work of Art in the Age of Mechanical Reproduction," Benjamin theorizes this aesthetic experience and refers to it as an "aura." According to him, the effect is informed by a nostalgia for the unity of the art object, by a desire to rediscover the object's original use value in the face of a mode of production that had already been transforming the creative process into a fragmented albeit collective assembly (p. 224). Fredric Jameson succinctly captures and elaborates Benjamin's use of the term "aura" in a manner that appropriately describes Darío's declarations above:

Aura for Benjamin is the equivalent in the modern world, where it still persists, of what anthropologists call the "sacred" in primitive societies; it is in the world of things what "mystery" is to the world of human events, what "charisma" is to the world of human beings. In a secularized universe it is perhaps easier to locate at the moment of its disappearance, the cause of which lies in general technical invention, the replacement of human perception with those substitutes for and mechanical extensions of perception which are machines. ("Versions of a Marxist Hermeneutic," p. 76)

By claiming that his works resemble the presumably autonomous literature that had been produced in a bygone era, Darío provides his works with an aura that highlights their rare value. It is from this perspective that we should recognize the extent to which the poet's language of sanctity, refinement, and selectiveness functions to advertise his books as if they were priceless heirlooms from a happier more prosperous time. For Darío, this retrospection facilitates a compensatory imaginary in which an idealized preindustrial world is invoked in order to counteract the artist's loss of social status and his weakened position vis-à-vis the modern production of literature. At the same time, such nostalgia is meant to provide the poet's readers with the aesthetic means by which they could ignore their inclusion in the workplace and simultaneously savor their distance from it. Through this tacit agreement between the poet and his reading constituencies, two conceptualizations of aesthetic distancing conveniently overlap. When he characterizes his book as complete, sacred, and valuable, Darío calls for a return to unmediated modes of production as an antidote to the modern worker's or, to be more precise, the poet's alienation from the products of his or her labor. Even though this imaginary is only viable after the fact, that is to say, after this alienation has already manifested itself in the workplace, it still satisfies the desire on the part of Darío's readers to ignore their relationship to that workplace while they are at leisure. Clearly, this mutual compensation takes place through consumption: the poet courts his readers' good taste since they are potential "customers" who will acquire his "priceless" books. Through such purchases, these readers define themselves on the basis of their power to acquire what the poet advertises as unique and incomparable.[2]

In "Palabras liminares," Darío illustrates the notion of the artist as the ordained mediator of a divinely inspired art by alluding to a sacred space of literary production. Through the only direct reference in this text to the act of writing, Darío associates his poetry with the writing of a monk:

Yo he dicho, en la misa rosa de mi juventud, mis antífonas, mis secuencias, mis profanas prosas. Tiempo y menos fatigas de alma y corazón me han hecho falta, para, como un buen monje artífice, hacer mis mayúsculas dignas de cada página del brevario. (A través de los fuegos divinos de las vidrieras historiadas, me río del viento que sopla afuera, del mal que pasa.) (p. 8)

[I have pronounced, in my youth's rosette mass, my antiphons, my sequences, my profane prose. Time and less weariness of the soul and heart have I needed, in order to, like a good craftsman-monk, make my capital letters worthy of each page of the breviary. (Through the divine fires of the storied stained-glass windows, I laugh at the wind that blows outside, at the evil that passes by.)]

In this imaginary scene, writing takes place inside a monastery. The monk's work harkens back to an age in which there are no mechanized mediators between the monk and the letters he draws on the pages of the missal.[3] To underscore the self-sufficiency of his work even further, the poet/monk dramatizes his isolation from society by laughing at the wind and evil that blow outside. This mocking gesture privileges the secure sanctity of the interior over the natural ("viento") and unnatural ("mal") inconsistencies of the exterior.

Herbert Marcuse has studied this desire for an internal refuge and posits this space as a locus of resistance to the rest of civilization. It is worthwhile examining what he calls "affirmative culture" because it elucidates some of the psychological consequences of bourgeois social practices:

By affirmative culture is meant that culture of the bourgeois epoch which led in the course of its own development to the segregation from civilization of the mental and spiritual world as an independent realm of value that is also considered superior to civilization. Its decisive characteristic is the assertion of a universally obligatory, eternally better and more valuable world that must be unconditionally affirmed: a world essentially different from the factual world of daily struggle for existence, yet realizable by every individual for himself "from within," without any transformation of the state of fact. ("The Affirmative Character of Culture," p. 95)

In Marcuse's view, the artist *asserts* that a better world exists within. Accordingly, affirmative culture liberates the individual from within so that there is no direct conflict with the exterior. Hence, liberation does not take place through social upheaval but by means of a process of cultural refinement that privileges the ennobling pursuit of ideal beauty (p. 103). From this perspective, culture does not describe society or any group inside it but refers instead to an acquired understanding of one's worth: "Culture means not so much a better world as a nobler one: a world to be brought about not through the overthrow of the material order of life but through events in the individual's soul" (p. 103). Advocating a similar pursuit of nobility, Darío asks in "Palabras liminares":

¿Hay en mi sangre alguna gota de sangre de Africa, o de indio chorotega o nagrandano? Pudiera ser, a despecho de mis manos de marqués: mas he aquí que veréis en mis versos princesas, reyes, cosas imperiales, visiones de países lejanos o imposibles: ¡qué queréis! yo detesto la vida y el tiempo en que me tocó nacer. (p. 9)

[Is there in my blood some drop of African, or Chorotega or Nagrandano Indian blood? That could be, in spite of my marquis' hands: but behold you see in my verses princesses, kings, imperial things, visions of far-off or impossible countries: What do you wish! I detest the life and time in which I happened to be born.]

The poet praises his hands over the rest of his sociobiological constitution because they can, figuratively speaking, produce a transformative art that elevates him above the tangible and the mundane.[4] The emphasis on the hand as the means of transformation recalls the previous commentary on the ritualized manual labor of the poet/monk. More interesting, though, is the notion that his hands, vital tools for his trade, are the very elements that he associates with an imagined aristocracy and that he compares unfavorably with his own ethnicity. Although his art is not explicitly conflictive, it is still subversive. Declaring an unequivocal hatred for his life and time, Darío scorns his surroundings and resolves a contradictory existence by celebrating an imaginary and aristocratic social order. During this celebration, "humanity becomes an inner state" (Marcuse, p. 103). In "Palabras liminares," Darío rejects the social in the advice he offers a "silvano":

La gritería de trescientas ocas no te impedirá, silvano, tocar tu encantadora flauta, con tal de que tu amigo el ruiseñor esté contento de tu melodía. Cuando él no esté para escucharte, cierra los ojos y toca para los habitantes de tu reino interior. ¡Oh, pueblo de desnudas ninfas, de rosadas reinas, de amorosas diosas! (pp. 10–11)

[The uproar of three hundred geese will not prevent you, sylvan, from playing your enchanted flute, providing that your friend the nightingale is pleased with your melody. When he isn't there to listen to you, close your eyes and play for the dwellers of your interior realm. Oh, village of naked nymphs, of rosy queens, of loving goddesses!]

Despite disturbances from the outside, the Sylvan's music is still audible to an audience within.

Darío's construction of the *reino interior* in these prologues does not imply a flight from social issues. On the contrary, in a more psychological as opposed to institutional view of the expression "revolution from within," Darío resolves his confrontation with an undesirable existence by assimilating and restructuring the social order through the practice of his art. "He apartado asimismo . . . ," he writes in "Dilucidaciones," "mi individualidad del resto del mundo, y he visto con desinterés lo que a mi yo parece extraño, para convencerme de que nada es extraño a mi yo" [I have similarly distanced my individuality from the rest of the world, and have impartially seen what to my "I" seems strange, in order to convince myself that nothing is strange to my "I"] (p. 12). Here resides the elitism in Darío's poetics. His wish to isolate himself from the outside world does not mean that he rejects his agency. Sylvia Molloy describes Darío's assertiveness when she notes how the poet projects "un yo voraz que, al proyectarse en lugares y personas, los despoja de sus características propias para transformarlos en aspectos de ese yo" [a voracious "I," which, on projecting itself upon places and persons, strips them of their own characteristics in order to transform them into aspects of that "I"] ("Conciencia del público y conciencia del yo en el primer Darío," p. 449). As in "Palabras liminares," his strategy in "Dilucidaciones" involves incorporating and recasting the world in his own image. In its almost complete transfiguration of the social into artistic representation, strategies of affirmative culture inform the hegemonic development of Darío's "I." It follows, therefore, that if revolution is concerned with changing the social order, then Darío's promotion of art and the imaginary over an external reality is truly radical.

Darío constructs his imagined space of literary production in order to champion the supreme authority of his published works. To achieve this goal, he deliberately scorns in "Palabras liminares" the forces of the marketplace. The poet declares: "Yo no tengo literatura 'mía' – como lo ha manifestado una magistral autoridad – para marcar el rumbo de los demás" [I do not have "my" literature – as an eminent authority has expressed – in order to mark the direction of the rest] (p. 8). When he refuses to serve as the leader of a literary movement or to offer his writings as models for a literary assembly line, Darío flaunts his personal uniqueness as well as that of his work. Like the preindustrial labor of the poet/monk that executes letters by hand, he claims to produce literature that is neither shared nor mediated. Describing the ownership of his writing in terms reminiscent of a feudal mercantilism, he warns others: "quien siga servilmente mis huellas perderá su tesoro personal y, paje o esclavo, no podrá ocultar sello o librea" [whomsoever subserviently follows my footsteps will lose his personal treasure and, be he page or slave, he will not be able to hide his seal or livery] (p. 8). In other words, those who attempt to fashion their literature along the lines of his texts stand to forfeit their own originality or creative freedom. Furthermore, those who copy what the poet has written in their texts cannot disguise their indebtedness to him nor, specifically, the brands ("sello o librea") that distinguish their literary labor as his property.

Consequently, almost any suggestion that his literary production should enter the marketplace meets with the poet's adamant disapproval. In a severe criticism of aesthetic theories in the marketplace, Darío writes in "Dilucidaciones": "Estamos lejos de la

conocida comparación del arte con el juego. Andan por el mundo
tantas flamantes teorías y enseñanzas estéticas. . . . Las venden al
peso, adobadas de ciencia fresca, de la que se descompone más
pronto, para aparecer renovado en los catálogos y escaparates
pasado mañana" [We are far from the known comparison between
art and games. So many brand-new theories and aesthetic teach-
ings make their way through the world. . . . They are sold by weight,
seasoned in fresh science, from which it rots soon enough, to
appear refurbished in the catalogues and shop windows the day
after tomorrow] (pp. 11–12). According to him, the marketplace
naturally devalues the work of art by commodifying it, releasing it
to market forces in which intertextual processes disturb the purity
of its internal production. "Disposal over material goods is never
entirely the work of human industry and wisdom, for it is subject to
the rule of contingency" (Marcuse, p. 89). In Darío's view, this rule
of contingency opens the literary work to the exigencies of less cul-
tured readers and writers (or consumers) and threatens to destroy
the greatness of his solipsistic, literary practice.

In light of the threat to the complete ownership of his works and
their mode of production, Darío refuses in "Palabras liminares" to
formulate a manifesto. As far as the production of literature is concerned, the manifesto becomes a license, a type of primitive copy-
right stipulation that governs the imitation of the original work.
From Darío's perspective, it may be said that the manifesto encourages the unregulated multiplication of works that would still carry
his trademark ("sello o librea"). In *Las contradicciones del modernismo*, Noé Jitrik uses the word "marca" to describe both the
inscription and trademark in the works of the *modernistas*:

Y ya que hablamos de "marca" – palabra que viene no por casualidad
ya que se trata de escritura – señalemos que la "originalidad" lograda
con el esquema productivo modernista es como la "marca de fábrica",
lo distintivo en toda la diversidad, en ese mundo infinito de la diferencia realizada, la unidad fundamental en la diferencia. (p. 7)

[And since we already speak of a "brand" – a word that comes not by
accident since it has to do with writing – let us point out that successful "originality" in the *modernistas*' production scheme is like a "trade-

mark," distinctiveness in diversity, in that infinite world of accomplished difference, fundamental unity in difference.]

To arrest this unregulated reproduction of his art, Darío formulates "Palabras liminares" as an antimanifesto, a declaration of the futility – "ni fructuoso ni oportuno" [neither fruitful nor opportune] (p. 7) – of artistic imitation and of Darío's refusal to place the fruit of his hermetic intellectual labor on the market. The first two clauses of the antimanifesto dissuade the consumer from copying Darío's works by denouncing the lack of preparation among Spanish American artists. Darío states his unwillingness to establish his work as an original model "por la absoluta falta de elevación mental de la mayoría pensante" [because of the absolute lack of mental elevation by the thinking majority] (p. 7) and "porque la obra colectiva de los nuevos de América es aún vana, estando muchos de los mejores talentos en el limbo de un completo desconocimiento del mismo Arte a que se consagran" [because the collective work of America's initiates is still unfounded, with many of the most talented in the limbo of a complete ignorance of the same Art to which they consecrate themselves] (p. 8). The third clause stymies all attempts at imitation by advocating the rule of no rule – "una estética acrática" [an anarchic aesthetics] (p. 8); since no model can be imposed, no imitation will ensue. In "Dilucidaciones," Darío reaffirms his stance claiming that there are no schools, only poets (p. 15).

Yet the antimanifesto contained in "Palabras liminares" seems to contradict the fact that in 1894, two years prior to the publication of *Prosas profanas,* Darío had written, with Ricardo Jaimes Freyre, probably the most cited manifesto of the *modernista* movement: the editorial remarks that inaugurated the first issue of the *Revista de América.* This publication's manifesto – beginning with its title, "Nuestros propósitos" [Our purposes] – documents an unbridled spirit of unity, equality, and preparedness. Its mood varies considerably from the one that Darío expresses in "Palabras Liminares," where he decries the immaturity of Spanish American art. The poet's awareness of the appropriate time and place for the manifesto explains this apparent contradiction. In other words, that

Darío wrote a manifesto two years before he publicly disclaimed the authority of this literary form does not amount to a contradiction in his aesthetics. The difference between the editorial comment, "Nuestros propósitos," and "Palabras liminares," lies less in their overt aesthetic claims than in the political economy – in Ensenzberger's sense – of their writing spaces.

According to Angel Rama, what Darío disclaimed was not the markt itself. Rather, he sought to blame the amateurs in the market for disturbing "el funcionamiento correcto del mercado literario dificultando la consecución de la secreta ambición de todos: la profesionalización del escritor" [the correct functioning of the literary market creating obstacles for the attainment of everyone's secret ambition: the writer's professionalization] (*Los poetas modernistas en el mercado económico*, p. 9). Hence, the generic awareness and interpellation of a reading public by means of the strategic acceptance or rejection of the *reino interior* is a crucial factor in the writer's professionalization. For Kimberly W. Benston, "the self of reputation commodifies identity, readying it for exchange in the public commerce of social power. But it is successfully launched into circulation only when etherealized as the 'something' of a nonreciprocal private self-enrichment" (p. 439). It is with such awareness of his reading public that Darío prefaced his work either at the inception of a new review or at the beginning of his book. In the final analysis, the *reino interior*'s exclusivity constitutes a persuasive form of advertising.

I have argued that as an imagined site of literary production, the *reino interior* in Darío's prologues functions as a strategy to interpellate a particular reading constituency. Yet, this personal appeal is not the only level of engagement with society that appears in these texts. Because I am interrogating a signifying language that is unavoidably composed of competing agendas propelled by varying degrees of political consciousness, I am obliged to take into account such ambivalent forms of engagement, including the ones that the *modernistas* inadvertently recorded in their works. For instance, in the most hermetic, imaginary space that Darío describes – the poet/monk's workshop in "Palabras liminares" – the social inevitably manifests itself in the construction of this closed realm, despite the efforts of its creator to safeguard this interiority. By the very attempt to spurn and/or reconstruct the social, the external is reconfigured, internalized in order to affirm the *reino interior*'s exclusivity. As I illustrated earlier, the reader can assume that when the poet/monk laughs at the exterior through ("a través de") the stained glass windows, the laugh penetrates the windows to mock and scorn the exterior. This interpretation suggests that there is a definite line of demarcation between a personal interior and a social exterior; in this view, the stained glass windows constitute nothing more than the *reino interior*'s periphery, the very boundaries of the poet/monk's language and artistic work. Falling in line with the escapist detachment hypothesis, this analysis reinforces the contention that the poet/monk's posture is defensive and completely adverse to any dialogue with the exterior.

However, the poet/monk's laugh may also be interpreted as a gesture that the "vidrieras historiadas" [storied stained-glass windows] mediate – that is to say, the stained-glass windows communicate disdain and ridicule by means of ("a través de") the inscriptions drawn on them. It is not arbitrary that these windows are fashioned for internal consumption only. In keeping with the ways in which stained-glass windows facilitate readings from within an enclosed space, the inscribed panes invoke an imaginary that is solely accessible to those who frequent or dwell in this internal realm. Nor is it coincidental that these panes simultaneously emblematize the poet/monk's distancing from the exterior. This aloofness should be taken not as a systematic and absolute avoidance of the social but as an ideological engagement with it through an empowering aesthetic practice. "What is represented in ideology is . . . not the system of real relations which govern the existence of individuals," Althusser succinctly states, "but the imaginary relation of those individuals to the real relations in which they live" ("Ideology and Ideological State Apparatuses," p. 165). As the emblem of an attitude toward society, as the site through which affirmative culture is reproduced, the *reino interior* does not denote flight. Rather, it establishes a language that its creators employed both to express opinions about their professional status and social prestige and to offer a critique of Spanish American societies in the name of aesthetic ideals which they, in the final analysis, were intent upon promoting.

The reino interior *as critical trope: A case study*

The *reino interior* is not only a conceptual site of literary production but a discursive field that has provided critics with opportunities to address and debate a variety of social issues. For example, there is a general consensus that Julián del Casal (1863–1893) suffered an unbearable existence because he had been born in the wrong time and place and that his literature represented attempts to combat this anxiety-ridden placelessness. When they examined his work, the Cuban poet's contemporaries often alluded to a personal malaise that they implicitly associated with his loss of status – a predicament that he endured, as it were, because of his family's financial decline and eventual bankruptcy (see José Antonio Portuondo, "Angustia y evasión de Julián del Casal" and Julio de Armas, *Casal*).[5] According to them, Casal sought through psychological and intellectual resources to rectify a social displacement: the art that he created was meant to compensate for his disenfranchisement and that of the class to which he belonged. Marcuse has studied these sorts of compensation and asserts that

one of the decisive social tasks of affirmative culture is based on [the] contradiction between the insufferable mutability of a bad existence and the need for happiness in order to make such existence bearable. Within this existence the resolution can only be illusory. And the possibility of a solution rests primarily on the character of artistic beauty as *illusion*. (pp. 118–19)

In the criticism on *modernismo*, attempts to determine the nature of the confrontations between the psychological and the social have made it possible, for instance, to liken Casal to the poet and protagonist of Darío's "El rey burgués," a figure who is relegated to the status of a lifeless, bourgeois collectible because he is obliged to earn his keep. Through such approaches, generic distinctions between biography and literary texts can be and, indeed, were eliminated by Darío, Henríquez Ureña, Portuondo, and others so that Casal's poems came to be considered clear, unmediated reflections of an inner turmoil. It is worth noting that in these assessments, through which the *reino interior*'s walls were rendered transparent and penetrable by a critical practice, there was no debate among Casal's contemporaries about the appropriateness of using the poet's life as a signifier for social unrest, no hint that his poetry could be anything but a direct link between personal anguish and the contradictions in his society. There was, in other words, a great deal of investment in affirming that Casal's life and work were symptomatic of his own as well as of Cuba's internal conflicts. This collective, discursive elaboration of the poet's *reino interior* allowed these artists and intellectuals to clarify their positions in Cuban cultural politics at the turn of the century.

The reason for turning my attention to Casal's first critics is to supplement the theoretical elaborations of the *reino interior* above with an analysis of how these critics constructed this discursive space. I am interested, therefore, in interrogating a critical practice, in examining the ways in which the language that was used to invoke the poet's suffering was also being employed to articulate particular political and cultural agendas. In her article on Casal's "Bustos," a series of literary portraits that was not compiled until after his death, Agnes Lugo-Ortiz points out that biographical writing transforms the body into "una zona de lectura" [a reading zone] and the biographer into its most knowledgeable reader (p. 397). Such approaches to Casal's interior realm also constitute *una zona de escritura* [a writing zone]. In my "case study" (and I employ the term not to promote Casal as emblematic of all *modernistas* but to suggest that similar methods may be employed to interrogate the types of *reino interior* that have been ascribed to them), I analyze how the poet's critics described his *reino interior*, that is, how they established connections between Casal's imagination, his literary production, and the social conditions that required the poet's imaginary resolutions in the first place.

However, before examining this practice among Casal's first critics, it will be necessary to highlight the features of the *reino interior* that shape their discourse. A frequent tendency in the literary criticism on Casal had been to reconstruct his ego by imputing particular meanings to it. Such reconstructions display the extent to which the language that was used to invoke the poet's *reino interior* facilitated a versatile discursive field, appropriately structured for critics to "diagnose" and debate Casal's and Cuba's internal contradictions coincidentally, yet sufficiently flexible for them to propose personal resolutions to those conflicts. In *Civilization and Its Discontents* (1930), Freud argues that the ego only appears to be autonomous and that it "seems to maintain clear and sharp lines of demarcation" (p. 13). Further investigating these appearances, he goes on to assert that these lines shift and that the ego itself is subject to growth and transformation. Central to the validity of these observations is the role of Freud's interpretive methods. According to him, psychoanalytic research has made the delineation of these borders an area for future research. Moreover – and for the purposes of this study – his understanding of the value of psychoanalysis for the study of pathologies is illuminating because it theoretically validates the kind of interpretive work that Casal's critics authorized themselves to practice. Freud writes:

Pathology has made us acquainted with a great number of states in which the boundary lines between the ego and the external world become uncertain or in which they are actually drawn incorrectly. There are cases in which parts of a person's own body, even portions of his own mental life – his perceptions, thoughts, and feelings – appear alien to him and as not belonging to his ego; there are other cases in which he ascribes to the external world things that clearly originate in his own ego and that ought to be acknowledged by it. Thus even the feeling of our own ego is subject to disturbances and the boundaries of the ego are not constant. (p. 14)

But who, one might ask, had been responsible for drawing the lines between the ego and the external world "incorrectly"? Herein lies the authority that the psychoanalyst and interpreter assume; furthermore, the need to correct and redraw these lines attests to the fundamentally dialogical nature of their interpretive practices. The resemblance between Freud's observations and those of Casal's critics resides in their narrative omniscience and in the manner in which they identify internal conflicts and posit their resolutions. For Casal's critics, this practice involved revealing the constitution of his ego and determining its boundaries by naming what was peculiar and/or alien to it. They based their authority, in other words, on defining the extent to which the boundaries of Casal's ego were "not constant." Although my comparison between Freud's theoretical observations and the interpretive practices of Casal's critics point to the existence of an incipient psychoanalytic approach to the poet's work, what I am most interested in illustrating are the social reasons that these critics offered in order to explain Casal's discomfort.

Casal's critics postulated that specific contradictions embedded in Cuban colonial society had produced a psychological imbalance in the poet. For example, in his review of *Hojas al viento* (1890) – Casal's first book of poems – the highly respected Cuban philosopher Enrique José Varona took the opportunity to define the work of the literary critic. According to his article, the critic "necesita conocer, indagar o suponer" [needs to know, investigate, or suppose] the relationship between the author and his environment (*Julián del Casal: Prosas 1*, p. 26). These three positions and activities vis-à-vis a body of knowledge outline the coordinates of a critical practice. Varona elaborates further on the value of these coordinates when he argues in the following sentence that it is only through them that it was possible to comprehend how Casal's book was the result of "un talento real y de un medio completamente artificial" [a real talent and from a completely artificial medium] (p. 26). The philosopher then proceeds to theorize this paradox, claiming that this artificiality derives from an unusual preference for verbal signs over the reality to which they refer (p. 27). It is illuminating to note in Varona's analysis the manner in which a psychological and cognitive space furnishes the site where Casal's "artificial" methods, namely his preoccupation with the French literature of the period, confront his "real" surroundings in Cuba (p. 27). Yet what is truly striking about these observations is not only Varona's coupling of falsity with the literature that Casal read but his claim that there is a connection between this cosmopolitan cultural literacy and neurosis:

Nuestra sociedad – adviértase que no decimos nuestro país – está condenada, por causas muy fáciles de determinar, a la imitación; que es la atmósfera donde se asfixia más fácilmente la originalidad. Es decir, a ser reflejo pálido de otras más ricas, más cultas y sobre todo, porque esto es aquí lo esencial infinitamente más numerosas. Son por todo ello entre nosotros plantas del todo exóticas el *mundanismo*, la literatura decadente y otras preciosidades y melindres sociales, que pululan en los salones selectos y semi-selectos de París. Esto no es decir que no tengamos personas muy cultas, muy elegantes y hasta muy refinadas. Hablamos del tono general de nuestra sociedad. En este ambiente, los jóvenes con tendencia al *neurosismo*, que leen libros franceses o sus malas imitaciones madrileñas, no encuentran el alimento que necesita su imaginación, sino exagerado [sic] las proporciones de las cosas, y desfigurándolas del modo más cómico. (pp. 27–8)

[Our society – be advised that we do not say our country – is condemned, by very easily determined causes, to imitation; which is the atmosphere where originality is most easily suffocated. That is, to be a pale reflection of richer and more cultivated ones and, above all, because herein lies the essential thing, infinitely more numerous. *Worldliness*, decadent literature and other fineries and social affectations that teem in the select and semi-select salons of Paris are for all that completely exotic plants among us. This is not to say that we do not have very cultivated, very elegant and even very refined persons. We are speaking about our society's general tone. In this ambience, young people with *neurotic* tendencies, who read French books and their bad imitations from Madrid, do not find the nourishment that their imagination requires, but exaggerate the proportions of things, and disfigure them in the most comical way.]

Varona does not directly state that Casal is neurotic but implies that the poet had to have overcome this condition in order to produce his convincing literature (p. 28). Central to the philosopher's thoughts on neurosis, however, are two issues that ought to be emphasized. The first deals with artistic creativity. According to Varona's criteria for a literature that best corresponds to the aspirations of preindependent Cuban society, a clear boundary distinguishes "imitación" (a propensity toward the acceptance or imposition, as the case may be, of external cultural references due mainly to Cuba's colonial status and cultural politics) from "originalidad" (a completely autochthonous and autonomous writing practice). This stark, binary opposition establishes a frontier that divides creativity into two areas of aesthetic choices that are ultimately linked to the sovereignty of a national literature or set of literatures. For the philosopher, imitation is a clear sign of infirmity. The second issue establishes an ambiguous connection between neurosis and reading because reading, as Varona formulates it, either causes or remedies this imbalance. Once again, it depends on the choice of literature. On the one hand, Varona argues that this cosmopolitan literacy can worsen a preexisting mental disorder; on the other, he approaches the same disorder with therapeutic advice and claims that an undernourished imagination can be reinvigorated by a regime of local, that is, non-European influences. In the final analysis, what accounts for this imbalance among young Cuban artists – and this is the principal shortcoming that Varona authorizes himself to critique – is their marginal relationship to the production of a truly national literature. Toward the end of his mostly positive evaluation of Casal's work, Varona summarizes his stance by maintaining that "Julián del Casal tendría delante una brillante carrera de poeta; si no viviese en Cuba" [Julián del Casal would have ahead a brilliant career as a poet; if he did not live in Cuba] (p. 29).

Casal died from an aneurysm at the age of thirty. News of the poet's death inspired a flurry of articles about his life and work. Three of them, by Justo de Lara, José Martí, and Rubén Darío, reiterate what Varona had pointed out as Casal's displacement by conflating the poet's anguish and a debilitating colonial situation. Eight days after Casal died, Lara recalled the poet's troubled existence as typical of those artists who, unable to pursue their vocation in Europe, must tolerate a basic lack of appreciation for their work at home. Explaining why going abroad becomes attractive to those who find themselves in this predicament, Lara implies that the plight of artists like Casal resulted from a fundamental incompatibility, an internal contradiction between an art that expressed the metropolis' maturity and sophistication and a colonial environment in which artistic development was being retarded by an undesirable relationship with the metropolis:

En este país todo el que aspire a algo más que la posesión de bienes materiales, y hasta aspirando sólo a esos bienes, todo aquél que desea gozar por ellos del bienestar físico que ofrecen los refinamientos de la civilización en otras tierras más adelantadas, ha de ser necesariamente un descontento. Pero cuando se siente en el cerebro aquel *algo* de que hablaba Chénier; cuando se sabe que hay lugares en el mundo en que manejar muy bien una pluma vale, por lo menos, tanto como vender azúcares o despachar arroz, y desde luego es más honroso, entonces el desencanto se convierte en desesperación. (p. 35)

[In this country all who aspire to something more than the possession of material goods, and even in aspiring only to those goods, all those who wish to enjoy through them the physical well-being that the refinements of civilization in more advanced lands offer, must necessarily be discontented. But when one feels in the brain that *something* about which Chénier spoke; when one knows that there are places in the world in which handling a pen very well is worth, at least, as much as selling sugar or dispatching rice, and of course is more honorable, then the disillusionment turns into desperation.]

Cuba's status as a Spanish colony provides the subtext for Lara's discussion of Casal's mental health. In the critic's view, Casal suffered from the realization that his art could be appreciated in places to which he had no access; or, from a related point of view, that he was producing work in and for a land that could not esteem it. Lara's juxtaposition of good writing and agricultural development alludes to debates throughout Latin America at that time about the incursions that economic life, mostly referred to as "utilitarianism," was making on domestic privacy, leisure time, spiritual life, and so on. Lara's position, however, is ambiguous at first. Despite the sympathetic tone with which he describes Casal's talent, he maintains that the poet's role as the creator of an art befitting more advanced lands had to be subordinated in a "country" that was still in the throes of its struggles for political and economic independence. Casal's displacement, therefore, derives from a failure to align his poetry with the national desire for autonomy; his interest in the cosmopolitan was a practice that the *independentistas* could not afford in their struggle to assert the primacy of their local struggles. Needless to say, this incommensurability is feasible only if one accepts the premise that the colonized nation already possesses an appropriate, that is, a mature and autonomous, literary voice that artists like Casal simply suppressed.

After listing the social reasons for Casal's personal suffering in this manner, Lara narrows his critical focus and assumes an even harsher tone in his recollection of the poet's solitude:

su vida tenía que ser la que fue y poseyendo una vocación tan absolu-ta e irresistible, poeta en Cuba sin conformarse a ser jamás otra cosa, tenía también que ser ante todo, un misántropo, una víctima con-stante del horrendo desequilibrio entre sus aspiraciones y su carácter y el carácter y las aspiraciones de cuantos le rodeaban. Será duro decirlo, será triste, pero es la verdad. Para su familia, para sus amigos, para la literatura cubana que aún podía esperar de su talento mejores frutos, la muerte de Casal es horrible. Para él es lo mejor que ha podi-do pasarle. No era un joven lleno como todos los demás, de esperan-zas y de ilusiones. Era un cenobita, solo en medio de todo un pueblo. (p. 36)

[his life had to be the one that it was and possessing so absolute and irresistible a vocation, a poet in Cuba without ever settling to be some-thing else, he also had to be above all, a misanthrope, a constant vic-tim of the horrid imbalance between his aspirations and his character and the character and aspirations of all who surrounded him. It will be hard to say it, it will be sad, but it is the truth. For his family, for his friends, for a Cuban literature that could still expect greater fruits from his talent, Casal's death is horrible. For him it is the best thing that could have happened to him. He was not a youth like all the rest, full of hopes and dreams. He was a cenobite, alone amidst an entire people.]

For Lara, Casal's unreasonable insistence on becoming a poet in Cuba and doing so in the face of other more urgent demands for his energies define Casal's misanthropy and cenobitism, tenden-cies for which death could be the only resolution.

Writing from New York (*Patria*, October 31, 1893), Martí evalu-ates the anomaly that his compatriot had been more familiar with the latest currents in France than with the events that took place around him in Cuba. He writes that Casal died "de su cuerpo endeble, o del pesar de vivir, con la fantasía elegante y enamorada, en un pueblo servil y deforme" [from his frail body, or from the grief of living, with elegant and enamored fancy, among a servile and deformed people] (p. 25). Martí then contrasts the unfortu-nate circumstances of Cubans under Spanish colonial rule with the rest of America, where "la gente nueva" flourish and insist on improving the quality and condition of their literature and politics. For Martí, Casal's work reflected these high standards, and it was for this excellence that he had gained recognition throughout the Americas. Blaming the adverse effects of colonial rule for the poet's psychotic conduct (and indirectly commenting at the same time on his own exile in the United States), Martí declares:

> Murió el pobre poeta y no le llegamos a conocer. ¡Así vamos todos en esta pobre tierra nuestra, partidos en dos, con nuestras energías regadas por el mundo, viviendo sin persona en los pueblos ajenos, y con la persona extraña sentada en los sillones de nuestro pueblo propio! Nos agriamos en vez de amarnos. Nos encelamos en vez de abrir vía juntos. Nos queremos como por entre las rejas de una prisión. ¡En verdad que es tiempo de acabar! (p. 26)

> [The poor poet died and we did not get to know him. Thus we all proceed in this wretched land of ours, split in two, with our energies dispersed throughout the world, living without personhood among distant peoples, and with the stranger seated in our own people's armchairs! We get bitter instead of loving one another. We become jealous instead of opening paths together. We love each other as if between prison bars. Truly it is time to end it!]

Being split in two – emptied of one's personality abroad and colonized at home, falsely imprisoned by local disunity – fully captures Martí's and Casal's displacements under colonialism. The fundamental and ironic distinction between both poets, however, lies in Martí's physical exile, a distance that ultimately did not prevent the vast majority of his critics from considering his writings patriotic. By contrast, Casal's exile is internal, and the success with which he was able to participate in a cosmopolitan literary discourse worked against him because it was used as evidence by critics to label the poet not only less patriotic than Martí but also deeply deluded and eccentric. In this early appraisal, Martí presages the manner in which his literature and Casal's were to be eventually historicized.[6]

In June of the following year, Darío wrote to Enrique Hernández Miyares, *La Habana Elegante*'s publisher, submitting his contribution to what he perceived as a general hastiness to categorize Casal's work. In his letter, Darío reiterates the Cuban poet's discomfort: "Yo me descubro respetuoso ante ese portentoso y desventurado soñador que apareció, por capricho de la suerte, en un tiempo y en un país en donde, como Des Esseintes, viviría martirizado y sería siempre extranjero" [I respectfully bare my head before that mighty and misadventured dreamer who appeared, by fortune's caprice, in a time and country in which, like Des Esseintes, he would live martyred and would always be foreign] (p. 32). Darío's laudatory critique corroborates Lara's and Martí's analysis of Casal's internal exile and explicates the latter's tormented existence by invoking particular psychosomatic symptoms:

La vida de Casal he dicho que fue una vida de martirio: la imposible realización de un ideal que se levantaba sobre todas las fases de la sociedad presente; (Casal nunca despertó de su sueño, no *quiso* nunca despertar); la enfermedad, los cilicios, la túnica ardiente de sus nervios, que ponían en su ser físico el germen de una muerte segura y pronta; por último, el veneno, la morfina espiritual de ciertos libros que le hicieron llegar a sentir el deseo de anonadamiento, la partida al país del misterio, o a cualquier parte que no fuese este pequeño mundo: *Any where out of the world!* (p. 32)

[Casal's life, I have said, was a life of martyrdom: the impossible realization of an ideal that rose above all phases of present society; (Casal never awoke from his dream, he never *wanted* to awaken); the illness, the hair shirts, the burning tunic of his nerves, that placed the germ of a sure and prompt death in his physical being; lastly, the poison, the spiritual morphine of certain books that made him come to feel the desire for annihilation, the departure to the land of mysteries, or to any place that was not this puny world: . . .]

This hyperbolic statement emphasizes Casal's constant physical discomfort. The reference to hairshirts and especially to a "túnica de nervios" centers this discussion on the poet's psychosomatic reactions to his living martyrdom. In the Nicaraguan's eyes, the dreaming that allowed Casal to separate his mind from his body is not a negative quality but a defiantly romantic one. Casal had been a martyr because he dared to imagine and be the receptacle for "la imposible realización de un ideal." Also significant in Darío's analysis is the way in which he describes Casal's literary taste (the assimilation of the foreign) as if it were a self-inflicted poisoning or drug overdose.

Yet Darío's comments on Casal must also be evaluated as they pertain to the former's interest in promoting *modernismo*. Ever attendant to the literary movement's momentum, Darío underscores the resonance of Casal's work in Europe and the Americas. He mentions that Menéndez y Pelayo considered Casal the first of Cuba's poets and that Verlaine thought him significant enough to merit his critique. Despite this recognition – or perhaps because of it – Darío insists that Casal "es un ser exótico" [is an exotic being] in Spanish letters and wonders what his fortune would have been had he been born in Paris (p. 32). With respect to the importance of solidifying Casal's fame, however, Darío advises:

En cuanto al poeta, al artista, hay que recoger, que compilar su producción, hacer la edición definitiva de su obra, dar a conocer al excelso mártir de su propio genio. Si no lo hace hoy Cuba, la generación de mañana lo hará. O se hará en otro país de América. Porque, en verdad te digo, un viento nuevo se siente venir sobre el alma de estas naciones, y los hijos de nuestros hijos se regocijarán en la luz. (p. 35)

[With respect to the poet, to the artist, it is necessary to collect, to compile his production, make a definitive edition of his work, acknowledge the sublime martydom of his own genius. If Cuba does not do it today, tomorrow's generation will. Or it will be done in another American country. Because, in truth I tell you, one senses a new wind overtaking these nations' soul, and the children of our children will rejoice in the light.]

Should it be compiled, published, and placed in archives, Casal's literary production would facilitate a bridge between his self-consuming intellect and the nation. Even though he objectifies Casal's work, focusing attention on his so-called self-destruction, Darío still considers the poet's contributions essential reading for future generations. In his concern for posterity, Darío considers the Cuban's writings tangible proof of nationhood and regionalism.

That the conflictive interior/exterior paradigm of Casal's besieged ego helped to structure a critical language resurfaced a few years after the poet's death, when M. Márquez Sterling in 1902 and Pedro Henríquez Ureña in 1914 informed their readers that

El Fígaro, the review for which they both published their articles on Casal, had celebrated its annual pilgrimage to the poet's tomb. Lara, Martí, and Darío had substantiated their analyses of the poet's *reino interior* by juxtaposing Casal's psychic life and Cuba's colonial condition. In Márquez Sterling's and Henríquez Ureña's articles, the figure of the poet's tomb provides a rhetorical polarity analogous to the *reino interior*'s manichean separation between the interior and the exterior. These critics, however, distinguish between a lost, valuable art embodied by Casal's works and the contemporary decadence and impoverishment of Cuban literature; they (and *El Fígaro*) employ Casal's tomb rhetorically in order to ground their critique of Cuban culture in nostalgia.

Márquez Sterling criticizes independent Cuba's lack of appreciation for the arts by recalling the site of the poet's remains. He facilitates a critique based not only on retrospection but on an unfavorable comparison between Cuba and the rest of Spanish America as well. Recalling how Casal and his art were superfluous to Cuba during his lifetime, Márquez Sterling argues that "para nosotros, un poeta como Casal era un exceso" [for us, a poet like Casal was an excess] (p. 40). Although he concurs with Lara's earlier claim that Casal's art was premature for the cultural politics of a colony struggling for nationhood, Márquez Sterling goes further and implies that it was the public which had not been prepared to understand and support the poet's works. By contrast, he urges young artists to imitate Casal's excellence, claiming that

fuera de Cuba, en la inmensidad sudamericana, en donde vive y prospera tanto poeta medianejo, su obra fue más preciada, su nombre obtuvo más gloria, y acaso ejerció un influjo de aquí apenas nos damos cuenta. Allá, el arte tiene campo, aquí el arte es una mentira. Allá la obra tiene su valor, el mérito tiene su premio, como la religión su altar sagrado. (p. 40)

[outside of Cuba, in the South American immensity, where many a mediocre poet lives and prospers, his work was more esteemed, his name obtained more glory, and perhaps exercised an influence about which we here are scarcely aware. Over there, art has room, here art is a lie. Over there the work of art has its value, merit has its reward, just as religion its sacred altar.]

Like Darío's concern for the posterity of a literary movement, these arguments and urgent tone are meant to stimulate national and regional literatures through the production of which writers and their reading constituencies could recognize themselves.

In "Ante la tumba de Casal," Henríquez Ureña bemoans the fact that Cuban literature prior to independence had fallen into oblivion. Even though he wrote his article twelve years after Márquez Sterling's, Henríquez Ureña invokes Casal's tomb and returns to the distinction that the former made between a forgetful Cuba and its more respectful neighbors. The need for reassessing Casal and appreciating his value comes to the fore when Henríquez Ureña asserts that the times had changed: "Cambiaron los tiempos; todo se transformó; cambió, entre otras cosas, la orientación literaria, y no para bien" [Times changed; everything was transformed; literary orientation, among other things, changed, and not for the best] (p. 41). Like Márquez Sterling, Henríquez Ureña also insists that Casal's works be considered literary models for the future. Analogous to those that preceded them, these critics found that the most effective way to couch their critiques of Cuban culture had been to set up a conflictive paradigm based on incompatibilities between an internal realm, albeit a posthumous one, and the rest of society.

In this chapter, I have looked at the *reino interior* as a conceptual site of literary production and as a discursive field through which turn-of-the-century critics began to institutionalize new exegetic practices. Both approaches to this internal space illustrate how Darío and Casal's critics meant to establish firm boundaries between an inviolable interior and a threatening exterior. Not only did this spatial polarity facilitate a discourse about pure art and privilege, it provided its creators with the means by which their interpretations and cultural literacy could be linked to the promotion of nationalisms and regionalism throughout Spanish America. Because of their difficult survival in the marketplace, the *modernistas* – as both the producers and critics of their own literature – were fascinated by the *reino interior* because it could represent their own troublesome status and subject positions. This trope made it possible for them to define and defend their own indispensability to Spanish American societies.

3

Poetry and the performance of cultural meaning
Darío's "Salutación del optimista"

The purpose of this chapter is to explore how certain *modernista* poems may be read as performed invocations of Spanish American and pan-Hispanic culture. In evaluating nineteenth-century representations of the region's culture, Jean Franco and Doris Sommer emphasize the importance of narrative in the construction of national and transnational identities. For Franco, these narratives were "simples alegorías" in which the intellectual did little to camouflage his own protagonism in the literature that he wrote ("Cultura y crisis," p. 414). Placing greater emphasis on writers as political leaders, Sommer points out that many of the region's authors (of romance) were also "the fathers of their countries, preparing national projects through prose fiction, and implementing foundational fictions through legislative or military campaigns ("Irresistible Romance," p. 73). Although narrative was undoubtedly effective in promulgating particular social imaginaries, poetry was also a frequently employed expedient of cultural meaning. For example, some of Darío's pre-1888 poems, like "Colombia," "Montevideo," "A Bolivia," "A la República Dominicana," and "Unión Centroamericana," indicate that he had been making the same kind of successful association between art and politics (cultural diplomacy) that the writers/statesmen of Spanish America's first novels had drawn. A poem that belongs to this group and one which in fact helped to launch Darío's career in Chile was "Canto épico a las glorias de Chile." This poem shared the first prize in a poetry competition that took place in 1887 (Ellis, pp. 11–12). Similarly, "Desde la pampa" (*El canto errante*) and "Himno de Guerra" eulogize Argentina and Nicaragua, respectively, by providing these nations with discourses reminiscent of the epic poems and ballads of the Middle Ages. But the poem among these that makes the grandest gesture toward imagining a supranational, trans-Atlantic Hispanism is Darío's "Salutación del optimista" (*Cantos de vida y esperanza*). Darío read this composition at the Sesión Solemne of the Ateneo de Madrid in 1905, where – as José María Vargas Vila, who witnessed the poem's recitation, claims – it was meant to redress the lingering "abulia" or apparent indifference among Spaniards after they had lost their remaining overseas colonies to the United States in 1898.

In this chapter, I offer an interpretation of "Salutación del optimista" to elucidate the cultural work that Darío wanted the poem to accomplish. To appreciate texts like these that have been handed down from other historical periods, especially ones for which an influential public forum had been provided, it is necessary to explore their immanent meaning(s). My interpretation of the poem, therefore, is founded on two conceptualizations of performance that, when they are brought together in one critical exercise, illustrate some of the consequences of reading "Salutación del optimista" as an inscribed, cultural text on the one hand and as a performance of cultural meaning on the other.

My first definition of performance takes as its premise the understanding that today "Salutación del optimista" is read as a written composition that says something about the *modernistas'* politics of cultural *rapprochement* with Europe at the turn of the century. An initial glance at the poem suggests that the utopian message it contains is straightforward: the poetic voice cajoles its addressees into sharing a nostalgia for empire and offers discursive strategies for (re)obtaining this grandeur. Yet, despite the consistency of these strategies, it remains unclear whether the optimism that the poetic voice represents as a personified Hope – "la divina reina de luz" [the divine queen of light] – facilitates or interrupts the poem's political message. Homi K. Bhabha refers to such instances of interruption as "double-writing or dissemi-*nation*," and he refers to the dual modes of representation that actualize them as the "pedagogical" and the "performative" (p. 299). By "pedagogical," he calls attention to a manipulative ideology of culture that summons itself into existence: "The pedagogical founds its narrative authority in a tradition of the people, described . . . as a moment of becoming designated by *itself*, encapsulated in a succession of historical moments that represents an eternity produced by self-generation" (p. 299). The "performative," by contrast, intervenes in the trajectory between the community's initial point of departure toward consciousness and its arrival at that utopian state; it "introduces a temporality of the 'in-between'" (p. 299). In other words, at any given moment, the pedagogical is disturbed by an internal difference, by an otherness and particularity that is neither the community's moment of genesis nor its fulfillment. The performative displays the pedagogical's structural deficiency; in poststructuralist discourse, it designates the impossibility of a permanent and pure meaning.

The second use of the term "performance" that interests me takes as its point of departure the more traditional significance of the word: Darío's public reading of "Salutación del optimista." The poet read his composition before an audience consisting mainly of intellectuals, poets, statesmen, journalists, entrepreneurs, and the like. This recitation might appear to be a passive form of political engagement, but it is not difficult to ascertain in this public reading the cultural significance of Darío's role as provider, performer, and custodian of an imagined community's social memory. When he undertakes this cultural work, more specifically, when he posits Spain's foundational legends as the principal heritage of the entire Hispanic community, Darío raises an important question with respect to the integrity of national patrimonies at that time: did his deferential treatment of European origins signal a subservience to that tradition or did it constitute an appropriation of cultural artifacts for the Spanish-speaking cosmopolitan classes in America? Since it is impossible to recreate the precise contingencies of that recitation, I will furnish proof of the poet's presence and role in the poem itself – just as Franco and Sommer did when they illustrated the agency of nineteenth-century, Spanish American authors in both their narratives and their political lives. Hence, my second definition of performance elucidates the play between the poetic voice's omniscience and its self-referentiality in "Salutación del optimista."

The poem as cultural text

The ideological thrust of "Salutación del optimista" resides in the poem's repeated efforts to privilege a unique legendary history of the foundations of pan-Hispanic culture. In the creation of discourses on the origins of national and cultural communities, the role of ancestors is central to linking a symbolic past with a prescribed future. "Of all cults," observes Ernest Renan in a lecture that he delivered at the Sorbonne in 1882, "that of the ancestors is the most legitimate, for the ancestors have made us what we are. A heroic past, great men, glory (by which I understand genuine glory), this is the social capital upon which one bases a national idea" ("What is a Nation?" p. 19). Focusing on the relationship between cultural uniqueness and writing, Leopoldo Alas argues that the originality of the literary work should emerge from "los misterios de la herencia, en el fondo de la raza" [the mysteries of heredity, from the depths of the race] (pp. 232–3). Steeped in this atmosphere of respect for pure lineage, it is no surprise that the *modernista* poems that imagine a common patrimony claim for Spanish American nations and pan-Hispanism a heritage of sagas and eulogies that celebrate the unproblematic founding of those geographic and cultural spaces. However, as in any ideological endeavor, the *modernista* creation of a writing space did not occur in a historical vacuum. The search for an original or autochthonous expression was not only compromised from the beginning by an inevitable relationship with the past but especially, in the case of Spanish American literature at the turn of the century, by an engagement with those mostly European literary traditions that had already historicized and disseminated their foundational legends. Selective borrowing from external sources inheres in creativity, and the *modernistas* appropriated what was available in order to forge their conceptualization of an ideal nation or group of nations.

This reliance on European traditions to advocate a pan-Hispanic cultural agenda is a frequent practice in *modernista* literature. But it is not peculiar to the movement's construction of a social memory. Paul Connerton states that "all beginnings contain an element of recollection. This is particularly so when a social group makes a concerted effort to begin with a wholly new start. There is a measure of complete arbitrariness in the very nature of any such attempted beginning. . . . But the absolutely new is inconceivable" (p. 6). Relative autonomy, in short, is characteristic of all attempts at self-definition. In "Salutación del optimista," there is evidence of this compromised sovereignty not only because it repeatedly appears as explicit calls for cultural "reconciliation" with Europe; this relative autonomy is also constituted by attempts to avoid direct references to the history of defeat and loss that the poem suppresses in the name of aesthetic purity and political consensus. In this initial look at the performative in the poem, let us examine the rhetorical maneuvers that the poetic voice negotiates in order to safeguard and promote the integrity of its agenda.

Throughout the poem, the poetic voice intermittently engages in the defense or deployment of a glorious European past and its recorded legends.[1] And it is this mnemonic movement back and forth in order to idealize august traditions that woos the listening public into concurring with Darío's version of a transnational social memory. The first recuperative effort appears in the second stanza, when the poetic voice warns that invoking the glories of classical legends will circumvent the spiritual restraints that retard pan-Hispanism:

Pálidas indolencias, desconfianzas fatales que a tumba
o a perpetuo presidio condenasteis al noble entusiasmo,
ya veréis al salir del sol en un triunfo de liras,
mientras dos continentes, abonados de huesos gloriosos,
del Hércules antiguo la gran sombra soberbia evocando,
digan al orbe: la alta virtud resucita
que a la hispana progenie hizo dueña de siglos. (ll. 12–18)

[Pallid indolence, deathly mistrust who to the tomb
or to perpetual imprisonment you condemned noble enthusiasm,
soon you will see the dawn breaking in a fanfare of lyres,
while two continents, enriched by glorious bones,
evoking the great magnificent shadow of ancient Hercules,
proclaim to the world: lofty virtue revives
the Hispanic progeny that it made the ruler of centuries.]

The poetic voice personifies and rejects indolence and mistrust on the grounds that they neutralize the transnational impetus to reunite. Inspiring a sense of renewal, this voice announces the community's bright future by recalling a glorious past: the rising sun casts Hercules' shadow on the landscape of two continents and the bones of illustrious ancestors bridge and renew the life of the land in both Europe and the Americas. This figurative bridging of two land masses is crucial because it lays the discursive foundations of a politics of cultural "reunification" between both regions. To accomplish this end, the poetic voice invokes a history that is meant to unite these continents. Hence, the origin that the poetic voice signals in this stanza is located not in a period of pre-Columbian eminence nor even in the encounter between Spaniards and the indigenous people of the Americas in 1492 but much further back, in the foundational legends of Western civilization.

The rejuvenation of Hispanic culture in the context of this poem does not signal a return to all the old truths; future greatness is built upon recalling Spain's filial relationship with the Roman Empire. At the same time, the selection of classical legends to represent the genesis of the pan-Hispanic community is a complex and ambivalent strategy. As I mentioned above, the poetic voice ignores indigenous contributions to American culture and concomitantly cherishes a European heritage. Yet this move complicates the poem's representation of identity politics because its deferential treatment of Spain's past is double-edged. Although it may have provided patriotic Spaniards and their Spanish American supporters with motives for reminiscing about past glories, this treatment implicitly draws an analogy between Spanish America's descendance from Spain and Spain's from Imperial Rome. Consequently, by eliminating the indigenous – the very presence of whom helps to make America unique – from this preferred social memory, the poetic voice creates a homogenous community of nations on both sides of the Atlantic with equal claims to direct lineage from one source. Inadvertently proposed or not, this notion of sibling nations stands as a direct challenge to the hierarchy of the former Spanish Empire.

In the third stanza, the poetic voice renews its attack against the enemies of Hispanic glory. On this occasion, it perpetuates its authority in the first four verses by appealing for the elimination of all dissent. Gradually, its omniscience makes way for omnipotence:

> Abominad la boca que predice desgracias eternas,
> abominad los ojos que ven sólo zodiacos funestos,
> abominad las manos que apedrean las ruinas ilustres,
> o que la tea empuñan o la daga suicida. (ll. 19–22)

> [Loathe the mouth that predicts eternal misfortunes,
> loathe the eyes that see only ill-fated zodiac signs,
> loathe the hands that stone illustrious ruins,
> or the one that takes up torch or suicidal dagger.]

Up to this point in the poem, the poetic voice has announced the opening of a new discursive space rooted in old traditions. And, as if to purify the site, the omniscient voice demands a closure that would exile the prophets of doom and those disrespectful of an illustrious past. This definitive closure never occurs, however. At the critical moment when it suggests that a frontier between itself and its adversaries can be drawn, that a permanent suture enclosing a fixed identity may be possible, the poetic voice moves instead to rally its addressees by alerting them to the threat of unforeseen, impending dangers:

> Siéntense sordos ímpetus de las entrañas del mundo,
> la inminencia de algo fatal hoy conmueve a la tierra;
> fuertes colosos caen, se desbandan bicéfalas águilas,
> y algo se inicia como vasto social cataclismo
> sobre la faz del orbe. (ll. 24–7)

> [Muffled turbulences from the bowels of the earth can be felt,
> the imminence of something fatal today moves the earth;
> mighty behemoths fall, two-headed eagles disperse,
> and something like a vast social upheaval is begun
> on the face of the globe.]

These rumblings emblematize the first kind of problem that the *modernistas* encountered and attempted to overcome in the construction of a pan-Hispanic social memory. In texts that generically resembled national anthems, since they exalted the triumphant beginnings of various nations, Darío conjured the opposition, albeit the defeated or the political enemy, as figures of chaos and catastrophe against which he rhetorically rallied his readers and listeners in apocalyptic scenes. This shift in focus to an impending catastrophe or to adversity within is typical of prescriptive definitions of culture. Jameson observes with respect to class conflicts that "the political thrust of the struggle of all groups against each other can never be immediately universal but must always necessarily be focused on the class enemy" (*The Political Unconscious*, p. 290). This observation also rings true for the *modernistas'* efforts to define (pan-)Hispanic identities.

The rhetorical importance of the poetic voice's ability to recognize impending dangers is also evident in "Unión centroamericana." As far as his political activism was concerned, this poem is significant because Darío had been invited to work on plans for the political unification of that region. In the following excerpt from that poem, the poetic voice describes the disaster that threatened to befall a sleeping nation should it fail to be moved by patriotic cries:

Y si el caos social, si las naciones
en terrible marasmo,
no sienten palpitar sus corazones,
y dormitan sin fe, sin entusiasmo,
faltas de inspiraciones;
si a la voz del deber no dan oídos
ni a los gritos de aliento
de patrióticos pechos, encendidos
con el fuego de un puro sentimiento;
si a la palabra sordas se presentan
y a la luz de la santa poesía,
y a la razón, que es luz también, intentan
convertir en fantástica utopía;
entonces, que haya un alma gigantesca
que a los pueblos despierte de su sueño
y que con mano audaz salve la idea
que hace grande al pequeño. (*Poesías completas*, p. 202)

[And if social chaos, if nations
in terrible apathy

do not feel their hearts beat,
and they doze off faithlessly, unenthusiastically,
lacking in inspiration;
if to duty's voice they do not lend an ear
nor to shouts of encouragement
from patriotic breasts, ardent
with the fire from one pure sentiment;
if to the word they appear deaf
and the light of holy poetry,
and reason, which is light too, they endeavor
to change into a fabulous utopia;
then, let there be a giant spirit
to awaken peoples from their slumber
and with a bold hand rescue the idea
that makes the insignificant grand.]

These allusions to social discontents and to their urgent solutions through national and regional awareness and unification in this early poem illustrate that apocalyptic scenes are familiar tropes in Darío's poetry. F. Javier Ordiz Vásquez writes that from 1905 onwards – that is, beginning around the time Darío composed "Salutación del optimista" – such scenes became more frequent in the poet's work (p. 13). These powerful images of chaos and struggle are not mere biblical allusions but urgent reminders that the community's future lies at stake.

The apocalyptic in these poems also registers the presence of ongoing, historical antagonisms. In the politically charged field of cultural signification, the lack of textual representation can be considered the disastrous outcome of a discursive struggle to be heard and historicized. Because it is conjured in such general and even abstract terms, the threat of an apocalypse in "Salutación del optimista" may refer not only to the Spanish defeat in 1898 or to social unrest in Europe. The impending catastrophe that is described in this stanza metaphorically elaborates the presence of negative forces as seismic activity. As competition among groups destabilizes the land (the political scenario), the movement of the earth in the poem reveals the subterranean presence of dissent or thwarted textual representation. Muffled earth tremors that tumble the mighty and scare off two-headed eagles (icons of national and imperial sovereignties, and of the Hapsburg Empire in particular) predict disaster. In the use of this seismic imagery, it is noteworthy that Darío's choice of metaphor for social unrest bears a striking resemblance to the figurative tectonics that Karl Marx employed in a speech commemorating the anniversary of the *People's Paper* (April 14, 1856). In that speech Marx warns: "The so-called Revolutions of 1848 were but poor incidents – small fractures and fissures in the dry crust of European society. However, they denounced the abyss. Beneath the apparently solid surface, they betrayed oceans of liquid matter, only needing expansion to rend into fragments continents of hard rock" (*The Marx – Engels Reader*, p. 577). In both examples of seismic activity, the earth's sudden destabilization encourages the reader/listener to heed the prophecies and acknowledge the authority of the omniscient observer.

However, since the poetic voice in "Salutación del optimista" claims to describe the cultural origins of the Spanish American side of the Hispanic community, it is difficult not to assert that in the competition to privilege one history the attempted erasure of competing histories will ultimately manifest itself in the poem. Because of its almost universal defeat or, at an equally relevant level, because there were insufficient written accounts for it to enter and compete in national archives, indigenous contributions to the collective Spanish American memory are almost entirely absent in *modernista* texts. When there are references to the indigenous, these references are doubly mediated (see Gullón, *Direcciones del modernismo*, and Ordiz Vásquez, "La esperanza del apocalipsis en la poesía de Rubén Darío"). These illusions are not, as Brotherston suggests, as accessible or relevant to Spanish American projects of cultural autonomy as the language of European nationalisms. He argues that

at their most confident Darío and his contemporaries wanted the best of both worlds. As the direct heirs to the conquistadors they insinuated a closer claim than the Spaniards to Hispanic glory, at the same time as arrogating to the highest grandeur of their material past: the resplendent courts of Meso-America and the majesty of the Inca. (*Latin American Poetry*, p. 38)

Darío writes in "Palabras liminares": "Si hay poesía en nuestra América, ella está en las cosas viejas, en Palenke y Utatlán, en el indio legendario, y en el inca sensual y fino, y en el gran Moctezuma de la silla de oro" [If there is poetry in our America, it is in old things, in Palenke and Utatlan, in the legendary indian, and in the sensual and refined inca, and in great Montezuma of the golden chair] (*Prosas profanas*, p. 9). In general, even though these images of pre-Columbian America provide the poet with artistic material that is just as mediated as European cultural capital (the Indian appears legendary, the Inca is sensual and refined, and Montezuma is almost on equal footing with his golden chair), they have little or no rhetorical value in *modernista* representations of Spanish American culture. Although he essentializes the indigenous as the dark irrational other, Gullón senses and universalizes the counterhegemonic possibilities of unknown and ignored spaces in cultural signification:

El indigenismo es, sustancialmente, llamada a las fuerzas oscuras, irracionales, y por ahí enlaza con la corriente actual de retorno a la sombra. Es una constante del espíritu humano indestructible, latente en la dimensión más honda de él. Corriente antirracionalista que reaparece en pleno auge del positivismo, para compensar y equilibrar las consecuencias de ese auge." ("Indigenismo y modernismo," p. 272)

[Indigenism is, essentially, a call to dark, irrational forces, and in that way it is entwined with the current movement of a return to the dark side. It is a constant of the indestructible human spirit, latent in its deepest dimension. An antirationalist movement that reappears in positivism's full rise, in order to compensate and balance the consequences of that rise.]

While these terms recall the very prejudices that "buried" any attempt to represent the indigenous in the poem, they indicate how suppressed voices can also be recuperated and made to proffer their unofficial story.

In the rest of the third stanza, the poetic voice attempts to cut off all further reference to oppositional forces and returns to a defense of pan-Hispanic greatness by posing and answering two rhetorical questions:

> . . . ¿Quién dirá que las savias dormidas
> no despierten entonces en el tronco del roble gigante
> bajo el cual se exprimió la ubre de la loba romana?
> ¿Quién será el pusilánime que al vigor español niegue músculos
> y que al alma español juzgase áptera y ciega y tullida?
> No es Babilonia ni Nínive enterrada en olvido y en polvo
> ni entre momias y piedras reina que habita el sepulcro,
> la nación generosa, coronada de orgullo inmarchito,
> que hacia el lado del alba fija las miradas ansiosas,
> ni la que tras los mares en que yace sepulta la Atlántida,
> tiene su coro de vástagos, altos, robustos y fuertes. (ll. 27–37)

> [. . . Who is to say that the dormant sap
> will not stir then in the trunk of the giant oak
> under which the Roman she-wolf's teat was suckled?
> Who will be the weak-hearted one to deny Spanish vigor its muscle
> and to judge the Spanish soul wingless and blind and maimed?
> Neither is Babylonia nor Ninive buried in oblivion and in dust
> nor among mummies and stones does the sepulcher reign that the
> magnanimous nation occupies, crowned by unblemished pride,
> that locks its anxious sights toward the edge of daybreak,
> nor does the one that beyond the seas in which Atlantis lies buried
> has its chorous of off-shoots, tall, robust and strong.]

The questions that begin this section of the poem challenge the imaginary dissenter's opinion that the Roman contribution to Western civilization and, coincidentally, Spanish vigor have waned. Shifting its attention from the earth tremors of the previous lines, the poetic voice conjures images of rebirth and ascendancy by adding an organic dimension to its invocation of the telluric. In the first question, it associates Spain's lethargy at the turn of the century with the dormant sap of the giant oak that shaded the she-wolf that suckled Remus and Romulus, the founders of Rome; in the second, it refers to anyone who denies Spain's strength and resolve as cowardly. The poetic voice answers its own questions by providing renowned examples of the longevity of certain cultures: even though they may be buried under sediments of time and history, legendary communities achieve immortality because they can be reconstituted through active recollection – or, in other words, through critical and performed reconstitutions of the social memory similar to the one that the poem itself undertakes. At this point in the poem, pan-Hispanic unity is conceptualized in the text's most difficult hyperbaton. Spain, the generous nation crowned by unblemished pride, can still prevail if it decides to look toward a new dawn; meanwhile, beyond the Atlantic, the grave of Atlantis, this same nation thrives because it possesses its chorus of tall, robust, and strong "vástagos" or off-shoots. Part of the hyperbaton's complexity lies in the fact that it is charged not only with merging two continents but the past and the future as well. This trope's cultural work aptly illustrates Paul de Man's observation that the "reconciliation of modernity with history in a common genetic process is highly satisfying, because it allows one to be both origin and offspring at the same time" ("Lyric and Modernity," p. 183). Once again, the phenomena that surround this transnational awakening supersede the Atlantic. That Spanish America should be described as new growth from ancient though fertile soil illustrates the extent to which the transnational Hispanic promise is contingent on new lands of opportunity.

This organic image of pan-Hispanic unity is further developed in the following stanza. In this new section, after denouncing the incredulous and the weak, the voice commands the Hispanic peoples to unite:

Unanse, brillen, secúndense, tantos vigores dispersos;
formen todos un solo haz de energía ecuménica.
Sangre de Hispania fecunda, sólidas, ínclitas razas,
muestren los dones pretéritos que fueron antaño su triunfo.
   (ll. 38–41)

[Unite, shine forth, support one another, so many scattered powers;
Together form a single bundle of ecumenical forces.
Blood of fecund Hispania, sturdy, illustrious races,
reveal the gifts of old that were once your triumph.]

This command to unite ends in a bundle of sticks ("haz de energía ecuménica") – like the *fasces*, the insignia of the Roman Consul and later this century of some of Europe's fascist political parties – that symbolizes the community's energy and unification.[2] This process began in the third stanza as a biological and historical metamorphosis that originated in a dormant tree. By the end of the third stanza, the nation possesses its chorus of off-shoots that are transformed in the first verses of the fourth stanza into a compact collection of sticks. In the rest of the fourth stanza, the organic whole acquires religious connotations when the desire to (re)convene one people takes the form of an epiphany in which the weight of venerated traditions complements the promise of youth:

> Vuelva el antiguo entusiasmo, vuelva el espíritu ardiente
> que regará lenguas de fuego en esa epifanía.
> Juntas las testas ancianas ceñidas de líricos lauros
> y las cabezas jóvenes que la alta Minerva decora,
> así los manes heroicos de los primitivos abuelos,
> de los egregios padres que abrieron el surco prístino,
> sientan los soplos agrarios de primaverales retornos
> y el rumor de espigas que inició la labor triptolémica. (ll. 42–8)

> [May the old enthusiasm return, may the burning spirit return
> that will rain tongues of fire on that epiphany.
> Together joined ancient heads framed by lyrical laurels
> and young heads that noble Minerva decorates,
> so too the heroic souls of the first grandfathers,
> of the eminent fathers who opened the pristine furrow,
> listen to the field breezes of spring-times returned
> and the rustle of wheatheads that Triptolemus' labor began.]

This pentecostal scene links the ancient and the new. It alludes to a perfect spiritual union in which tongues of fire alight on the heads of gathered believers. The adorned heads of the ancients and those of bright youths (and also, by inference, Spain and Spanish America) are brought together in this celebration of unity. Gradually, this unity becomes so pervasive that it even encompasses communities at the threshold of Western civilization: the heroic souls of the earliest generations that tilled the land are remembered and made to perceive the breeze of Spring's renewal and the rustling of wheatheads to which Triptolemus' labor first gave rise.[3] The poetic voice not only stakes a claim on the future; it also recruits ancestors, thereby rearranging fundamental categories of time so that the community's destiny appears to continue a tradition of greatness.

In the final stanza, the poetic voice predicts a glorious future once the Hispanic peoples on both sides of the Atlantic have come together in spirit, desire, and language:

> Un continente y otro renovando las viejas prosapias,
> en espíritu unidos, en espíritu y ansias y lengua,
> ven llegar el momento en que habrán de cantar nuevos himnos,
> La latina estirpe verá la gran alba futura,
> en un trueno de música gloriosa millones de labios
> saludarán la espléndida luz que vendrá del Oriente,
> Oriente augusto en donde todo lo cambia y renueva
> la eternidad de Dios, la actividad infinita. (ll. 50–7)

> [One continent and another renewing old ancestral ties,
> united in spirit, in spirit and urges and tongue,
> behold the arrival of the moment when they must sing new hymns,
> The Latin stock will behold the great new dawn,
> amidst the thunder of glorious music millions of lips
> will greet the splendid light that will emerge from the Orient,
> an Orient where everything is changed and renewed
> by God's eternity, the never-ending activity.]

The joining of both continents recalls the poetic voice's previous attempt to envision the bountiful future that could result from such a partnership. In the verses above, this partnership portends glory for the Latin lineage by making it the first to contemplate a new dawn. The light of this new day appears from the East, the direction where Western civilization posits its ancient origin and from which the sun rises (and God's infinity renews itself) daily. The celebration of this epiphany terminates the ideological thrust of the poem because it marks the utopian moment of the community's self-realization. The grandiloquent crescendo of this stanza does not immediately allow the listener to question the proposed partnership. It seals the cultural union not only by considering the new dawn the uncontested domain of Latin peoples but also by identifying through an implicit comparison the Anglo-Saxon race as a common adversary. After 1898, Spanish America faced the threat of North American cultural and imperial hegemony. By then, British commercial and military interests had already been active in South America. At the same time, Spanish America's attitude toward North America was a great deal more complex than this fear of the north's hegemony. For example, in the realm of literary production alone, some readers may have already noted the resemblance in tone between "Salutación del optimista" and poetry from Walt Whitman's *Leaves of Grass*.[4]

The obstacles to signifying pan-Hispanism that Darío faced when he composed "Salutación del optimista" are as evident in the poem as they are in today's language of identity politics. So far, we have concentrated on the poem's explicit cultural agenda and have only intimated the subterranean presence of muffled voices in the text. Yet, as we shall now see, the representation of this agenda – that is, the poem's call for unity and its pursuit of that utopia – is compromised almost from the very start. In the course of emblematizing optimism as Hope, a profound moment of troubled meaning manifests itself in the revelation of this poetic object. Materializing in the poem as an emblem of communal desire that signifies and simultaneously exhibits the incompleteness of cultural meaning, Hope's shimmering appearance both fosters and stymies the invocation of a transnational identity. When Hope enters the scene in the following verses, the poetic voice describes it in a way that is meant to specify its essential nature; but, with the addition of each new qualifier, the object becomes even less tangible:

> se anuncia un reino nuevo, feliz sibila sueña
> y en la caja pandórica de que tantas desgracias surgieron
> encontramos de súbito, talismánica, pura, riente,
> cual pudiera decirla en sus versos Virgilio divino,
> la divina reina de luz, ¡la celeste Esperanza! (ll. 7–11)

> [a new realm is ushered in, felicitous sibyl dreams
> and in the Pandora box from which so many misfortunes emerged
> we suddenly find, talismanic, pure, gleeful,
> as only divine Virgil could say her in his lines,
> the divine queen of light, celestial Hope!]

Now, the wordiness of this description is not only characteristic of Darío's and the other *modernistas*' so-called penchant for sculpting their poetic objects. It is crucial to acknowledge (with hindsight, naturally) that this pleonasm is also representative of the basic, poststructuralist premise that meaning cannot be permanently designated. Tendencies toward verbosity in these texts, in other words, temporarily circumvent a signifying "failure" because the poetic object never fully captures meaning but approximates it. With respect to this study as a whole, this view allows me to assert that what critics traditionally perceived as evasion, superficiality, and art for art's sake had in all likelihood been informed by their observations that the *modernistas* did not (and could not) posit and specify pure meanings. Let us pursue this point further by illustrating the effect that Hope's properties have on the poem's ideological thrust.

A series of layered, literary references envelops Hope's "pure" meaning. The first allusion to the presence of intermediaries comes in the form of a dreaming sibyl. Sibyls – by some counts there were as many as ten or twelve – were prophetesses associated with various parts of the ancient world, such as Babylon and Greece. They were the forerunners of the more familiar muses. Legend has it that at night oracles were revealed to them, which they subsequently communicated to poets, priests, and others during the day. The sibyl's appearance in the poem clearly connects the land with prophecy and representation; its position, however, is also ambiguous. When the image of a dreaming sibyl abruptly follows on the heels of a new realm that is being announced, the relationship between prophecy and land implicitly authorizes the poetic voice as the mediator of cultural signification. But if the sibyl is the dreaming subject that objectifies the new kingdom, then the poetic voice risks losing its authority and becoming a part of the sibyl's dream.

The second layer that compromises meaning is Pandora's box. The "y" that introduces the box does not clarify whether or not the box, like the "reino nuevo," is the object of the sibyl's dream. What is noticeable, however, is that with the removal of one layer of textuality (the sibyl's dream) and then another (the lid, one assumes, on top of Pandora's box), the poetic voice employs the indexical "we" as it enters the poem to gaze upon Hope. At this critical moment, a third layer is used to conceal Hope: the voice and its listeners/readers perceive something that only one as divine as Virgil can utter. The first stanza, therefore, seduces the listener and reader into witnessing the absence of the signified, an absence that is quickly camouflaged by recourse to the revered authority of the Roman poet.

But even apart from the references that obfuscate it, Hope itself shimmers because of its qualifiers. While its adjectives attempt to concretize it, the poetic object persistently remains elusive and ambiguous. Hope is "talismánica, pura, riente." That it should be talismanic does not imply that it contains a single, pure meaning or, in other words, that it will have the same significance for all its listeners and readers. Hope's varied properties in "Salutación del optimista" are a statement on the process of signification in language itself. According to the *Diccionario enciclopédico de la lengua castellana*, there are three kinds of talismans: the astronomical (hence, Hope's qualification as "celeste"); the magical, in which superstitious words prevail; and a mixed group of barbaric names and signs. These three types vary in accordance with each one's proximity to privileged and accepted discourses. Despite the plethora of possible readings that radiate from it at any one moment, Hope, paradoxically, remains "pura." Consequently, the opportunity to conceive of a particular, uncontaminated meaning is retained, but the value that that unique meaning holds is complicated by its duplicity: Hope is also discovered laughing at the moment she is revealed in Pandora's box.

Despite its polysemy, Hope remains central to the poem's advocacy of pan-Hispanic optimism. Absent from all the intervening stanzas, the poetic object reappears in the poem's final two verses. Significantly, by returning to the scene before the act of self-naming, Hope facilitates this definitive utterance. The poetic voice begins the stanza by equating the completion of a pan-Hispanic union with a single language, spirit, people, and future and hails this union repeating the same verse that began the poem. This repetition, however, does not have the effect of the poem's opening salute. On this occasion, when the poetic voice calls for all the

Hispanic peoples to interiorize Hope – the missing ingredient –
the community names itself:

> Y así sea Esperanza la visión permanente en nosotros,
> ¡Inclitas razas ubérrimas, sangre de Hispania fecunda! (ll. 58–8)
>
> [And so may Hope be the permanent vision in us,
> Illustrious prolific races, blood of fecund Hispania!]

In this utterance, that is, in this completion of the ideological project through language, the community speaks its name, and, one
supposes, the poetic voice's prophecies begin to come true.

For so powerful and instrumental a cultural ideology as the self-
naming of a people, the less than politically activist sentiment of
hope in "Salutación del optimista" seems to offer an anticlimactic
end to a grand project. But, as it did in Europe, hope had special
resonances at the end of the nineteenth century in Spanish
America. It became a frequent reference in *modernista* poetics
because it attempted to compensate not only for the nebulous
vision of the future that modern socioeconomic forces had begun
to produce but also for the awkward social status of an *intelligentsia*
that was being obliged to find new ways to authorize itself and often
did so by advocating a social imaginary based on notions of
progress and optimism. At the same time, Hope denotes the very
limits of the poet's ability to engage its audience as well as entire
nations. Short of concretizing the utopian pan-Hispanic space
through immediate action, listeners and readers are left to ponder
and be inspired by hope, the catalyst of a subjunctive mood, one of
the strongest linguistic means of staking proprietorship over future
events.

The performance of cultural meaning

I have looked at the some of the ways in which "Salutación del optimista" registered the difficulties of signifying pan-Hispanic culture
in a written text. The reading that I undertook above had as its
object of inquiry the relationship between a particular cultural
agenda and its internal inadequacies. Because this poststructuralist

analysis stresses the impossibility of fixing a permanent pan-Hispanic meaning, its ability to elucidate the appeal and forceful-ness of Darío's political message is limited. In "Beyond Discourse-Analysis," Slavoj Žižek notes, referring to Laclau's and Mouffe's notion of "social antagonism," that "far from reducing all reality to a kind of language-game, the socio-symbolic field is conceived as structured around a certain traumatic impossibility, around a cer-tain fissure which *cannot* be symbolized" (p. 249). Clearly, fissures of this sort surfaced in the poem and manifested themselves in the text's cultural tectonics – that is, the rumbles and cracks caused by the muffled voices of the defeated and other dissenters, by the fig-urative elimination of the Atlantic, and most of all by the prescrip-tive conflation of Europe's past glories and Spanish America's promising future. Nevertheless, while phrasings such as Žižek's "traumatic impossibility" and Bhabha's "dissemi*nation* or double-writing" reinforce the validity of a poststructuralist logic, they are descriptive terms that cannot articulate the degrees of self-recognition and interpellation that initiatives such as "Salutación del optimista" offered its listeners. In other words, it is crucial to avoid the trap of ascribing this logic to Darío's intentions, that is to say, of proving that the poet wanted to *suspend* his message between an agenda that he pursued and an expression that consistently fell short of his goal.

To respect the historical circumstances of Darío's recitation, these critical approaches ought to be supplemented by greater attention to what messages remain immanent in the text even after its performance. "If the work no longer has meaning through ref-erence to a primary reality located elsewhere," Kimberly Benston rightly observes, "it has not suspended meaning as such but, rather, has relocated it as an immanent and even an essential property of the work – as the performative experience itself" (p. 440). In order to circumscribe and valorize this immanence, I examine parts of the text and reveal how the poet intervenes and alludes to his own indispensability in the course of promoting the poem's transna-tional cultural politics.

Upon recalling the auspicious occasion of his recitation of "Salu-tación del optimista" in Madrid in 1905, one may be tempted to perceive the poet's performance as an outmoded means of cultural expression and production. Even though the event may be considered one of the high points in the literary movement and a personal triumph for Darío's career, the recitation's contingencies have transpired. Nevertheless, the performative is still discernible in the text: the poetic voice regularly alludes to its own future self-fulfillment, and it is this thematization of oral expression and voice that most reveals the immanence of a united, pan-Hispanic community in the poem. When "Salutación del optimista" was performed, this repeated thematization took on an important metadiscursive function because it not only signaled Darío's role as the visionary advocate of a particular cosmopolitanism; it also highlighted the ways in which he could promote the autonomy of his art.

In the poem, the poetic voice summons the Hispanic *raza* and demands its attention before a discursive and political event that takes place by the end of the poem: the people's enunciation of its own name. This naming process begins in the first two lines of the poem when the poetic voice hails its audience:

> Inclitas razas ubérrimas, sangre de Hispania fecunda,
> espíritus fraternos, luminosas almas, ¡salve! (ll. 1–2)

> [Illustrious prolific races, blood of fecund Hispania,
> fraternal spirits, luminary souls, all hail!]

The omniscient poetic voice identifies its audience and salutes it grandly. The relationship between the exteriority of this voice and the manner in which it calls its addressees into existence is based on a reciprocity in which the salute posits a racial and spiritual kinship that the poetic voice claims to share. However, subsequent allusions to forthcoming and apparently different voices and modes of articulation suggest that the poetic voice oscillates between a desire for omniscience and the will to participate in the community's self-realization. These voices and modes of expression consistently materialize whenever figures for the pan-Hispanic people are employed. In the following example, a collective form of oral expression is thematized, and its mention coincides with the foundation of a profane paradise:

> Porque llega el momento en que habrán de cantar nuevos himnos
> lenguas de gloria. Un vasto rumor llena los ámbitos; mágicas
> ondas de vida van renaciendo de pronto;
> retrocede el olvido, retrocede engañada la muerte (ll. 3–6)

> [For the moment approaches when glorious tongues must sing
> new hymns. A vast rumble fills spheres; magical
> waves of life are suddenly being reborn;
> oblivion withdraws, death misled withdraws;]

The sound of hymns sung by a host of tongues produces a rumble that creates the timeless, spiritual space of the new community. New hymns – a reference in which the genesis of the *raza* is accompanied by the same kind of rejoicing that "Salutación del optimista" itself evokes – infiltrate spaces, recall past lives, and cause oblivion and death to retreat. Their rendition by "lenguas de gloria" identifies the event with the Day of Final Judgment. There are examples of other such conflations in the rest of the poem. In the second stanza, the rising sun that serves to dissipate a cultural and spiritual lethargy appears in "un triunfo de liras" (l. 14). Lyres are symbols of poetry *par excellence,* and their representation at this juncture also symbolizes a bid to champion the autonomy of a poetic expression. In the fourth stanza, in an epiphany that is meant to emblematize a new enthusiasm, "lenguas de fuego" (l. 43) descend as in the Pentecost, when Christ's disciples gathered and thus received the Holy Spirit. Similar to the poem's first lines, the voices that unite are sanctified by the elevation of the secular to the religious. In the last strophe, the thematization of the poet's and poetry's role in facilitating cultural unity resonates most. At the end of the poem, the transnational community congregates. According to the poetic voice, this unity will allow it to witness the moment in which new hymns or anthems will be sung and the day when it will gaze upon a new dawn; this perfect union is accompanied by "un trueno de música gloriosa" in which "millones de labios/ saludarán la espléndida luz que vendrá del Oriente" (ll. 54–5).

The same play between a voice that announces the approach and activity of another voice and then utters what the latter is supposed to say occurs in a very familiar text of the period in

Argentina. The following verses are taken from the Argentine National Anthem (adopted in 1813):

> ¡Oíd, mortales! el grito sagrado;
> ¡Libertad, libertad, libertad!
> Oíd el ruido de rotas cadenas
> Ved en trono a la noble Igualdad
> ¡Ya su trono dignísimo abrieron
> Las Provincias Unidas del Sur
> Y los libres del mundo responden
> ¡Al gran pueblo argentino, Salud!
> ¡Al gran pueblo argentino, Salud! (Reed and Bristow, pp. 27–32)

> [Listen, mortals! the sacred cry;
> Freedom, freedom, freedom!
> Listen to the sound of broken chains
> Behold enthroned noble Equality
> The United Provinces of the South
> have already established their honorable throne
> And the free men of the world reply
> To the great Argentine people, *Salud*!
> To the great Argentine people, *Salud*!]

In this excerpt of the anthem, as well as in all of "Salutación del optimista," an omniscient authority exists only to the extent that the act of self-naming is deferrable. This consistent recourse to a self-generating omniscience appears in some of Darío's other patriotic poems as well. In the following verses from "Canto a la Argentina" (1910), for example, the poetic voice calls attention to a shout ("el grito") that literally creates the Argentine landscape:[5]

> Oíd el grito que va por la floresta
> de mástiles que cubre el ancho estuario,
> e invade el mar; sobre la enorme fiesta
> de las fábricas trémulas de vida;
> sobre las torres de la urbe henchida;
> sobre el extraordinario
> tumulto de metales y de lumbres
> activos; sobre el cósmico portento
> de obra y de pensamiento
> que arde en las poliglotas muchedumbres;

sobre el construir, sobre el bregar, sobre el soñar,
sobre la blanda sierra,
sobre la extensa tierra
sobre la vasta mar. (*Canto a la Argentina*, pp. 7–8)

[Listen to the shout that floats above the thicket
of masts that cover the wide estuary,
and invades the sea; above the enormous *fiesta*
of factories trembling with life;
above the towers of the swelling city
above the extraordinary
commotion of moving metals and
lights; above the cosmic wonder
of toil and thought
that burns in the polyglot crowds;
above the constructing, above the toiling, above the dreaming
above the gentle mountains
above the wide earth
above the vast sea.]

Whereas the shout summons listeners, the enunciation remains at all times strategically above in order to frame the topography. In the examples above, the vision of an ideal, Hispanic community designates the role of its advocates and its own self-realization.

What appear as an immanent cultural agenda in "Salutación del optimista" are the moments when the people's self-enunciation coincides with the advocacy of a literary movement. These moments are not simply distinctions between form and content or messenger and message but contextualized examples of successful negotiations in which artists and intellectuals such as Darío were able to hinge the professionalization of their art on the promotion of a cosmopolitan cultural agenda. The shifts between the poetic voice's omniscience and its production of the indexical "we" attest to duplicitous postures in which the intellectual either objectifies from outside and above or speaks as a patriotic subject from within discourses on the nation or *raza*.

In his account of Darío's recitation of "Salutación del optimista," Vargas Vila writes that the poet received "un triunfo merecido y estrepitoso" [a worthy and resounding triumph] (p. 91). Today, it is still possible to illustrate the ways in which Darío's "Salutación del optimista" captures the difficulties involved in signifying Hispanic communities. At a basic level, the poem lays bare the issue of creating meaning through language: the inability to specify and name the object without having to resort to negotiations over the appropriateness of signifiers. With respect to the cultural text, this incapacity reveals the difficulties of arriving at a consensus on cultural signs and agendas before the figure of the community can be diffused, propagandized, and projected into the future. By contrast, the performance of cultural meaning provides an immanence that transcends textual representation. Through their craft of literature, their nostalgia for the Classical and Christian roots of western civilization, Darío and other *modernistas* furnished credible representations of the regional/national Hispanic space for a select public. Poems of this sort fulfilled a desire for transnational unity among Spanish and Hispano-American intellectuals, political leaders, and other members of the ruling classes.

4

Sculpting Spanish America
Rodó's *Ariel*

In "The Case of the Speaking Statue: *Ariel* and the Magisterial Rhetoric of the Latin American Essay," Roberto González Echevarría argues that José Enrique Rodó's *Ariel* (1900) sets the lead and tone for a tradition of essay writing in Latin America and that the fictionality and persuasiveness of this foundational text resides in its complex ventriloquism. With respect to generic precedents, the *maestro*'s (Próspero's) rhetoric is structurally reminiscent of Plato's dialogues. Yet because the text consists almost entirely of the farewell speech that a revered teacher delivers to his students, Rodó's essay attempts to produce a "dialogical effect" when in fact "there is no dialogical exchange in the essay" (p. 20). *Ariel* – a product of scribal culture – endeavors to communicate its messages as unmediated oratory. A more evident form of ventriloquism unfolds, however, as Rodó transmits his ideas through Próspero, who in turn emblematizes his discourse in the form of the exquisite albeit silent statue of Ariel next to him (p. 26). Although González Echevarría's arguments are persuasive, I would like to examine further a form of dialogism that the critic alludes to only as "the way in which these figures engage in a polemical interplay beneath the surface of the essay" (p. 19). I am referring to the essay's intertextuality. In *Ariel*, Rodó confidently enters into dialogue with the philosophical and political thought of his times. His intertextual practices do not represent an unreflexive incorporation of literary material. Nor do they constitute the relentlessly unilateral dependency on European literatures that Salinas and others identified as the principal feature of *modernista* aesthetics. The exclusive application of a "dependency theory" to Spanish American literature skews intertextuality in favor of a presumably mature and complete

European literature. Since this issue of cultural/intellectual progress and underdevelopment (or, in the language of the period, imitation) involves a determination in Spanish American letters of exactly who is assimilating whom and how, it behooves me to explore the cultural intertextualities that Rodó's essay actualizes. In this essay, Rodó purposefully borrows from European traditions and does so in order to create an original and, unavoidably, a relatively autonomous work of literature.

Ariel's canonization can be evaluated from two interpretive approaches that I employ in a complementary manner so that a more comprehensive, critical dialogue about the construction and naturalization of cultural icons may be undertaken. The first approach focuses on the essay's ideological content. At one point in his evaluation of Rodó's text, Carlos Martínez Durán asks a question pertinent to the essay's symbolism: "¿Conoce a fondo la juventud la simbología de Ariel y Calibán en Shakespeare, Renan y Rodó, y sus trasmutaciones para definir las sociedades, los pueblos, las naciones, el hombre mismo?" [Is the youth fully acquainted with the symbolics of Ariel and Caliban in Shakespeare, Renan and Rodó, and their transmutations for defining societies, peoples, nations, man himself?] (p. 84). His question is rhetorical; for he refrains from answering it and enters instead into a reflection on Latin American youth. Following González Echevarría's and Martínez Durán's signals, I concentrate on how Rodó appropriates and modifies specific discourses on aesthetics, class, and political freedom by tracing his incorporation and reelaboration of the three main characters from Shakespeare's *The Tempest* (1623) – Prospero, Ariel, and Caliban – through their mediation in Ernest Renan's version of the same characters in *Caliban* (1878), to their final manifestations in *Ariel*.

The other approach to the essay in which I am interested examines the ways in which Rodó promoted his text among writers, critics, and intellectuals. In these promotions, Rodó's language is often formulaic and collusive in tone, features that suggest that the essay's ideological content represents only part of the story about its canonization. *Ariel*'s rise to prominence is also based on the workings of a trans-Atlantic network of critics and their "public" writing spaces in magazines, reviews, and the like. To interrogate these foundational critical practices, I elucidate the activities that take place after the essay's publication – for the most part, the correspondence between Rodó and literary critics that facilitated and promoted *Ariel*'s propaganda. In his edition of Rodó's *Obras completas*, Rodríguez Monegal observes that the Uruguayan used his correspondence to cultivate an important "política literaria" [literary politics]: "La correspondencia era un arma formidable de un labor de proselitismo americanista, de su [Rodó's] milicia de América (como le gustaba decir)" [Correspondence was a formidable weapon in the labor of an Americanist proselytism, of his American soldiery (as he liked to say)] (p. 1319). In this respect, the attitude toward reception that the text demands of the reader may well have been primed not just by the text's dialogue with the reader but also, in the case of *Ariel*, by the readership and audience that its author and critics helped to create for the essay.

Cultural intertextuality

One way to trace the interconnectedness of *The Tempest*, *Caliban*, and *Ariel* is to explore how each text provides certain characters with liberty or deprives them of it. In *The Tempest*, there is an effective balance of power. Prospero is the former Duke of Milan and a magician who imposes his rule on the island where the drama unfolds. Ariel and Caliban are his servants: the first is a genie temporarily bound in obedient service to the magician, and the second is a "savage and deformed slave" (p. 95) who constantly complains about his master and, on one occasion, plots to murder him. In Shakespeare's drama, Prospero and Ariel control the destinies of all the play's characters through their combined magic. Prospero owes his extraordinary abilities to his books, to his theoretical understanding of magic. Caliban is aware of the power of these books because he warns his accomplices, Trinculo, the jester, and Stephano, the butler: "First to possess his books; for without them / He's but a sot, as I am, nor hath not / One spirit to command – they all do hate him / As rootedly as I. Burn but his books" (III, ii). Ariel, by contrast, complements the magician's knowledge with its ability to manipulate and transform the material world. The magician's verbal agreement to liberate the genie maintains this equilibrium. For every job well done, for every step accomplished in Prospero's plan, the magician greets the genie with variations of the same promise: "Thou shalt ere long be free" (V, i). Each reiteration of this promise serves to rekindle Ariel's desire for liberation, so that by continuously promising and postponing the genie's emancipation, the gratification of the desire to be free is perpetually imminent and at the same time elusive.

After he realizes his plan, Prospero keeps his word and frees the genie to the elements. When Ariel vanishes into the air, the verbal contract that maintains the power configuration is voided. Prospero's and Ariel's ability to keep the surly and belligerent Caliban at bay also secures the power equilibrium. Unlike the agreement that exists between the magician and the "airy spirit," Caliban's enslavement is definitive, nonnegotiable. The only hope for liberty that he entertains is that of killing Prospero and destroying the order that subjugates him. Notwithstanding, the only successful means of insurgency at the slave's disposal is his ability to use the language that Prospero and Miranda, the magician's daughter, taught him.

A common theme that runs through the three texts is the difference in the attitudes and responses of the subservient characters to their respective forms of bondage.[1] When the characters and their relationships with one another are appropriated and recast in *Caliban* and in *Ariel*, the price of liberty is established in accordance with the subservient characters' obedience or rebellion. In *Caliban* – his "Drame philosophique" – Ernest Renan modifies the relationships of Prospero, Ariel, and Caliban, invoking a discussion about class conflicts and democracy such as those so frequent around the end of the nineteenth century in Europe.[2] In Renan's appropriation of Shakespeare's play, Prospero regains control of his dukedom and continues to employ Ariel's services. Caliban, however, becomes a representative of the masses in conflict with the aristocracy. Like Caliban's subversion of Prospero's linguistic imperialism in *The Tempest*, the ability of Renan's Caliban to use the official language to his advantage takes on an explicitly ideological significance. Asked by Bonaccorso in *Caliban* if he has any enemies, Prospero replies: "Eh! pardon, j'ai Caliban. Ce misérable me doit tout. Quand je le pris à mon service, je lui appris la parole, créée par Dieu; il ne s'en est jamais servi que pour m'outrager" [Eh! forgive me, I have Caliban. That wretch owes me everything. When I took him into my service, I taught him speech, created as it was by God; he has never served but to insult me] (IV, iv). To this complaint about Caliban's rise to political power through language, Gonzalo (the wise counselor, the voice of reason in Shakespeare's play) adds his observations in clearly elitist terms: "Caliban, c'est le peuple. Toute civilisation est d'origine aristocratique. Civilisé par les nobles, le peuple se tourne d'ordinaire contre eux. Quand on regarde de trop près le détail du progrès de la nature, on risque de voir de vilaines choses" [Caliban, that's the people. All civilization is of aristocratic origin. Civilized by nobles, the people ordinarily turn against them. When one looks at the details of nature's progress from too close, one risks seeing some hideous things] (IV, iv). When Caliban eventually triumphs over Prospero, his class, and Ariel, his victory is informed by the former slave's recently and imperfectly assimilated discourses on civil rights:

J'y ai droit, à cette liberté! Autre fois, je n'avais nulle pensée; mais, dans cette plaine de Lombardie, mes idées se sont bien developpées. Les droits de l'homme sont absolus. Comment Prospero se permet-il de m'empêcher de m'appartenir à moi-même? Ma fierté d'homme se révolte. Je m'enivre de sa cave, c'est vrai; mais le premier crime des princes n'est-il pas d'humilier le peuple par leurs bienfaits? Pour effacer cette honte, il n'y qu'un moyen, c'est de les tuer; un pareil outrage ne se lave que dans le sang. (I, i)

[I have a right to that liberty! Formerly, I hadn't given it a thought; but, in this Lombardy plain, my ideas have developed well. Man's rights are absolute. How is Prospero allowed to prevent me from belonging to myself? My manful pride revolts. I drunken myself from his cellar, that's true; but isn't the main crime of princes that of humiliating the people with their kindness? In order to erase that shame, there is only one way, it's to kill them; an insult of this kind does not wash away except by blood.]

These words are supposed to represent the awakening political consciousness of the masses. Renan draws on Shakespeare's depic-

tion of Caliban's savagery, deformity, and enslavement and transposes this image to the ex-slave's newly assimilated discourses on
civic and democratic rights. Caliban expresses his incomplete
assimilation of this language by demanding his rights and, in the
same breath, by depriving his enemies of their basic right to live.

Caliban's speech exhibits the simultaneous, unstable fusion of
two competing discourses. In his essay, "Nationalism: Irony and
Commitment," Terry Eagleton juxtaposes these discourses as separate critical approaches to bourgeois society: "In the manner of
Enlightenment radicalism you can press for the revolutionary
extension of universal rights" (p. 31). Such a critique would forcibly
remind those in power of the disenfranchised. The other tactic,
according to Eagleton, would be that of Romantic radicalism: "you
can embrace the local, sensuously specific, and irreducibly individual and seek to shipwreck an abstract idealism on the rock of
the completely real" (pp. 31–2).[3] Caliban espouses a peculiar conflation of both discourses. Renan transposes this deformity to
Caliban's reign: when the former slave rises to power, he attempts
to do so by creating a new but eventually anarchistic bureaucracy.

In order to counterbalance Caliban's eventual rise to power,
Renan radically idealizes Ariel's servitude:

PROSPERO: Ainsi, mon Ariel, tu veux m'être toujours fidèle. Vingt
fois je t'ai dit: "Tu vas être libre, Ariel." Je te garde toujours.
ARIEL: (visible) Comme il vous plaira, seigneur. Que ferais-je de ma
liberté, si ce n'est de m'absorber dans les éléments dont vous
m'avez tiré. C'est par vous que j'existe. Je vous aime, et j'aime ce
que vous faîtes. (I, ii)

[PROSPERO: So, my Ariel, you want to be forever faithful to me.
Twenty times have I said: "You are going to be free, Ariel." I still
look after you.
ARIEL: (visible) As you please, my lord. What would I do with my
freedom, if not lose myself in the elements from which you drew
me. It is through you that I exist. I love you, and I love what you
do.]

At the end of the play, when Ariel and Prospero are defeated by
their own unpopularity with the masses, their magic (elitist politics) no longer seems to work. Having surrendered, Ariel reports

to Prospero: "O mon maître, notre art est vaincu; il est impuissant contre le peuple. Il y'a sûrement dans le peuple quelque chose de mystérieux et de profond" [Oh my master, our art is vanquished; it is powerless against the people. There is surely something mysterious and profound in the people] (IV, iv). It is at this point that the magician offers the genie its freedom. Replying that such freedom signifies its death, the genie delivers the final words of the play in a manner that opens the text to Rodó's subsequent reading and appropriation: "Je serai l'azur de la mer, la vie de la plante, le parfum de la fleur, la neige bleue des glaciers. Je ferai mon deuil de ne plus participer à la vie des hommes. Cette vie est forte, mais impure. Il me faut de plus chastes baisers" [I shall be the sea's azure, the plant's life, the flower's perfume, the glacier's blue snow. I shall say good-bye to no longer participating in men's lives. That life is strong, but impure. I have need of more chaste kisses] (V, ii). In Renan's play, the spirit is not absorbed into natural elements, as in *The Tempest*, but into a dimension of lyrical commonplaces. For the genie, its disappearance into the azure of the sea, a color so treasured by the *modernistas* and the Symbolists, implies not only freedom but also its reappropriation in certain literary forms and movements.

In *Ariel*, Rodó seeks to regain the classicist balance of power that Renan pessimistically abandons in *Caliban*. Próspero becomes an old and respected schoolmaster whose words of wisdom constitute the speech delivered to the students gathered in his study. Like Shakespeare's Prospero, Rodó's relies on books for his authority. Though he is physically absent as a figure in the text, Calibán and his deformity are repeatedly invoked as Ariel's antithesis. Rodó recaptures the genie – and thereby continues Renan's discussion of the conflictive relationship between class interests and democracy – by plucking Ariel from its deliverance to the azure sky in *Caliban* and recasting it in the form of an exquisitely crafted bronze figure that is meant to inspire Spanish America's youth. Rodó brings the lyricism of Ariel's *adieu* to bear upon his description of the statue. In this description, there is an interesting overlap between art and politics. Ariel's artistic form literally captures the virtues the statue is supposed to possess:

La estatua, de real arte, reproducía al genio aéreo en el instante en que, libertado por la magia de Próspero, va a lanzarse a los aires para desvanecerse en un lampo. Desplegadas las alas; suelta y flotante la leve vestidura, que la caricia de la luz en el bronce damasquinaba de oro; erguida la amplia frente; entreabiertos los labios por serena sonrisa, todo en la actitud de Ariel acusaba admirablemente el gracioso arranque del vuelo; y con inspiración dichosa, el arte que había dado firmeza escultural a su imagen, había acertado a conservar en ella, al mismo tiempo, la apariencia seráfica y la lealtad ideal. (p. 26)

[The statue, of true art, reproduced the airy spirit in the moment when, freed by Prospero's magic, it is going to hurl itself into the air so as to vanish in a flash. Wings spread; the light garb loose and floating, that the light's caress on the bronze damasked with gold; the ample forehead raised; lips half-opened by a serene smile; everything in Ariel's demeanor admirably revealed the flight's gracious impulse; and through fortunate inspiration, the art that had given sculptural firmness to its image, had managed to conserve in it, at the same time, an angelic appearance and ideal loyalty.]

Sculpture and casting are the mediums *par excellence* of Rodó's art of democracy. The material worth and the description of the statue are significant. The choice of bronze, a metal traditionally reserved for commemorating the influential and the powerful, corresponds to Rodó's idealization of the genie (see González Echevarría, pp. 26–7). When the statue is characterized as a "bronce primoroso" [exquisite bronze] (Rodó, p. 25), the adjective "primoroso" emphasizes in equal proportions the sublime beauty and expert craftsmanship of the statue. It appears that through his promotion of an exquisite art, Rodó attempts to establish a perfect balance between an aesthetic theory and its practice: he recuperates an equilibrium analogous to the combination of Prospero's theoretical magic and Ariel's practice of that sorcery in *The Tempest*. However, the description of the bronze figure contains another curious conflation. The art that gives Ariel its sublime form is simultaneously responsible ("había acertado a conservar en ella, al mismo tiempo") for depicting the figure's ideal loyalty. This particular double stroke – for "lealtad" may be read as artistic loyalty to form (realism) as well as personal obedience – is facilitated by the use of the chisel.

According to Próspero, there exists an "estética de la estructura social" [aesthetics of the social structure] (p. 49), a social hierarchy fashioned by exquisite design. In this order, the artist makes use of the chisel to accomplish an artistic and political project reminiscent of Homi Bhabha's "pedagogical" mode of cultural meaning: the transformation of Calibán from raw material – "símbolo de sensualidad y de torpeza" [symbol of sensuality and awkwardness] (p. 26) – into Ariel, the finished masterpiece. Eagleton refers to this kind of transformation as a process of self-realization:

The metaphysics of nationalism speak of the entry into full self-realization of a unitary subject known as the people. As with all such philosophies of the subject from Hegel to the present, this monadic subject must somehow curiously preexist its own process of materialization – must be equipped, even now, with certain highly determinate needs and desires, on the model of the autonomous human personality. (p. 28)

Próspero's pedagogy, in other words, is founded on preconceived notions of the "ideal" student. Moreover, toward achieving his teaching goals, Próspero almost always associates the chisel with the process of giving concrete and aesthetically refined form to intangible entities. For example, in his explanation of the value of Classical civilization, Próspero states that "Atenas supo agrandecer a la vez el sentido de lo ideal y el de lo real, la razón y el instinto, las fuerzas del espíritu y las del cuerpo. Cinceló las cuatro faces del alma" [Athens knew how to aggrandize at the same time the meaning of the ideal and of the real, reason and instinct, the spirit's forces and those of the body. It chiseled the soul's four faces] (p. 50). (Although bronzes are cast, and it is the mold into which the liquid bronze is poured that is sculpted, this technicality does not weaken Rodó's text, for there exists in Spanish the idiomatic expression "cincelar el bronce.") In light of this process, it may be said that Próspero's study is an art studio for the creation of cultural paradigms and that the chisel in this studio becomes the artistic and political means by which a manipulative ideology of culture fashions its model of social organization. In his conception of an aesthetic cultural order, Próspero maintains that there are models worthy of emulation. To support this view, he proclaims: "es . . . una necesidad inherente a la ley universal de *imitación*, si se la relaciona con el perfeccionamiento de las sociedades humanas, la presencia, en ellas, de modelos vivos e influyentes, que las realcen por la progresiva generalización de su superioridad" [it is . . . a necessity inherent in the universal law of *imitation*, if it is related to the perfection of human societies, that there be present in them lively and influential models, that may enhance them through the progressive spread of their superiority] (p. 98). Naturally, the cultural model that reigns supreme for the schoolmaster is the one that captures the genie in bronze: "Ariel es, para la naturaleza, el excelso coronamiento de su obra, que hace terminarse el proceso de ascensión de las formas organizadas, con la llamarada del espíritu" [Ariel is, for nature, the sublime crowning of its work, that brings to an end, with the spirit's beckoning, the ascending course of organized forms] (p. 148). But what does Rodó's argument gain by establishing Ariel, a beautifully crafted bronze statue, as the culminating figure of a process of aesthetic selectivity?

Rodó's idealization of Ariel's beauty continues Renan's struggle to reverse Caliban's rise to power through democracy. This idealization is the means by which class allegiances infuse cultural identity. In *Caliban*, Ariel's disappearance into a dimension of lyricism amid the anarchy of Caliban's reign reinforces Renan's urgent defense of high culture and its producers against the rise and spread of the bourgeoisie. The French thinker exacerbates the difference between idealism (Ariel's ethereal existence) and democracy by equating the latter with Caliban's materiality (tangible existence) and his excessive materialism (substantive needs). This conflation of materiality and materialism, incarnated in the figure of Caliban, supplies the key to understanding the allegorical function that Caliban and democracy assume in Renan's play. Próspero summarizes Renan's ideas on the threat that Caliban represented to society:

Piensa, pues el maestro [Renan], que una alta preocupación por los intereses ideales de la especie es opuesta del todo al espíritu de la democracia. Piensa que la concepción de la vida, en una sociedad donde ese espíritu domine, se ajustará progresivamente a la exclusiva persecución del bienestar material como beneficio propagable al mayor número de personas. Según él, siendo la democracia la entronización de Calibán, Ariel no puede menos que ser el vencido de ese triunfo. (p. 78)

[The master, of course, thinks that a great concern for the human species' ideal investments is completely opposed to the spirit of democracy. He thinks that life's conception, in a society where that spirit prevails, will progressively be adjusted to the exclusive pursuit of material well-being as a benefit reproducible for the greatest number of persons. According to him, democracy being Caliban's enthronement, Ariel cannot but be the defeated one in that triumph.]

This summary explains Ariel's defeat: the genie cannot triumph in the face of the rising tide of an exclusive dedication to material pursuits. Rodó distinguishes his text from Renan's by insisting upon Ariel's recuperation and recasting in the concrete form of a statue. By presenting Ariel as a refined cultural model with a material existence, Rodó indicates that he can tentatively accept Calibán's struggle for democracy. For, it must be remembered, Calibán symbolizes the initial stage, the raw material or "la arcilla humana" [human clay] (p. 147) that must be refined through a process of spiritual and cultural perfection. This tentative acceptance allows Rodó to express qualified appreciation for Calibán's deformities and his propensities toward rebellion. It permits him to historicize and contextualize within his argument an autochthonous expression of the struggle for democracy. Realizing that Renan's scorn for democracy is limited to the class concerns of an eclipsed, European aristocracy, Próspero defends Calibán's rebelliousness by declaring: "La obra de la Revolución . . . en nuestra América se enlaza además con las glorias de su Génesis" [The Revolution's work . . . in our America is intertwined moreover with the glories of its Genesis] (p. 79). Because it was responsible for the birth of the American nations, revolution justified the necessary ejection of imperial powers. Furthermore, Próspero promotes the need for a positive project that would transcend the initial moment of rebellion, thus reinforcing his role as schoolmaster: "Desde el momento en que haya realizado la democracia su obra de negación con el allanamiento de las superioridades injustas, la igualdad conquistada no puede significar para ella sino un punto de partida. Resta la afirmación" [From the moment when democracy will have accomplished its work of denial through the leveling of unjust hierarchies, that won-over equality cannot signify for it but a point of departure. Affirmation remains] (p. 80). In other words, to counterbalance Renan's pessimism and, by the same token, to consider the potential of an American democracy, the schoolmaster concludes that "sólo cabe pensar en la *educación* de la democracia y su reforma" [it is only fitting to think about democracy's *education* and its reform] (p. 91).

The originality of Rodó's essay lies in this objectification of democracy under the auspices of a pedagogical program; it inserts the concept of democracy in Próspero's art studio. Unlike Darío's attempts to discourage the imitation of his art, Rodó advocates civil and ethical codes of behavior inspired by the aesthetic experience of Ariel's ideality. Yet, even in his bid to return to the equilibrium of *The Tempest*, in his attempt to posit a new politically forceful aestheticism, Rodó overdetermines the usefulness of his pedagogy. At first, Próspero points out his students' need for guidance by claiming that "en sociabilidad, como en literatura, como en arte, *la imitación inconsulta* no hará nunca sino deformar las líneas del modelo" [in sociability, as in literature, as in art, *untutored imitation* will do nothing but deform the model's lines] (p. 104; emphasis added). In the context of the art studio, the necessity of a guiding hand is understandable. But Próspero exceeds his pedagogical function and his role as advising instructor by stating that "la multitud será un instrumento de barbarie o de civilización según carezca o no del coeficiente de una alta dirección moral" [the multitude will be an instrument of barbarity or civilization according to the lack or not of the coefficient of an elevated moral leadership] (p. 82). It is noteworthy that the schoolmaster sees the masses and not his pedagogical program as the instrument of social organization. In any case, Próspero transposes the "advisory" capacity of the teacher to the level of the state. In this transposition, Próspero establishes a new hierarchy, one that recalls Ariel's privileged position in the art studio:

El deber del Estado consiste en colocar a todos los miembros de la sociedad en indistintas condiciones de tender a su perfeccionamiento. El deber del Estado consiste en predisponer los medios propios para provocar, uniformemente, la revelación de las superioridades humanas, dondequiera que existan. De tal manera, más allá de esta igualdad inicial, toda desigualdad estará justificada, porque será la sanción de las misteriosas elecciones de la Naturaleza o del esfuerzo meritorio de la voluntad. Cuando se la concibe de este modo, la igualdad democrática, lejos de oponerse a la selección de las costumbres y de las ideas, es el más eficaz instrumento de la selección espiritual, es el ambiente providencial de la cultura. (pp. 92–3)

[The State's duty lies in placing all of society's members in indistinct conditions of their tendency toward perfection. The State's duty lies in predisposing the appropriate means to provoke, uniformly, the emergence of human superiorities, wherever they may exist. In such a way, beyond this initial equality, every inequality will be justified, because it will be the sanction of Nature's mysterious choices or the will's meritorious endeavor. When it is conceived in this way, democratic equality, far from opposing the selection of customs and ideas, is the most efficient instrument of spiritual selection, it is culture's providential milieu.]

According to Próspero, the state – like his art studio – can set up a certain goal ("la revelación de las superioridades humanas") and explain how it is to be achieved ("esfuerzo meritorio de la voluntad"). However, at the height of this assertion of his subjectivity and the projection of that subjectivity to the state's infrastructure, Próspero yields his agency to the unpredictability or contingency of Nature and providence. This rhetorical move is contradicted by the schoolmaster's earlier derogatory references to the phenomenon of chance. He rejects "la torpeza del acaso" [chance's awkwardness] because its blind force exposes the future to "los peligros de la degeneración democrática" [the dangers of democratic degeneration] (p. 81). That the new order should be informed and sanctioned by forces that are as ubiquitous as they are uncontrollable effectively erases the schoolmaster's role in his pedagogical design.

Paradoxically, the schoolmaster's attempted erasure of his own pedagogical role signals an important stage in Ariel's naturalization into a cultural icon and transcendence to social signification. Barbara Johnson refers to erasures of this kind, in which the producer (of poetry) tries to hide his or her own agency, as fetishization:

This obliteration and forgetting of the process of production and the consequent overestimation of the object produced, this erection of a fixed, statufied form as proof against mutilation and incompleteness, is characteristic of what both Marx and Freud have called fetishism. Both as a monument set up against the horror of castration and as a seemingly "mystical" product divorced from the work of its production, poetry – the potency and seemingly inexhaustible wealth of language – indeed reifies itself into a sort of linguistic fetish. (pp. 47–8)

Johnson's definition recalls Darío's desire to establish the incomparability of his literature and its separation from any acquirable means of production. As we have seen, his declaration of an "estética acrática" [anarchist aesthetic] reiterates his refusal to abide by the rules of the assembly line, so that when the work of the artist is enveloped by the *reino interior*, it becomes a ritual, a fetishized activity. Therefore, it is not surprising that the only guideline Darío proffers the artist is played out in the following quotation: "Y la primera ley, creador: crear. Bufe el eunuco. Cuando una musa te dé un hijo, queden las otras ocho en cinta" [And the first law, creator: create. Let the eunuch snort. When a muse bears you a child, may the other eight become pregnant] ("Palabras liminares," p. 11). With respect to the fetishization of the literary work, it is appropriate that in this formula a eunuch and his enunciation of an unintelligible sound should fill the cognitive space between the unconjugated injunctive to create and the subsequent inexplicable impregnation of the muses. In *Ariel*, the same kind of fetishization whereby the work is divorced from its production occurs both within and outside the essay. Up to this point, I have shown how the essay creates Ariel as a culturally significant "bronce primoroso" through a process of assimilation and idealization. But Ariel is depicted as more than just a statue or exhibition piece limited by decorative significance to a schoolmaster's book-lined study. Even though the art studio in which Próspero gives his speech presupposes an exclusive channel of communication between the schoolmaster and his students, the statue dominates the room not only as a numen (p. 25) – in this sense, "a 'mystical' product divorced from the work of its production" – but as a beautiful art object that displays an amazing vitality independent of its invocation by the schoolmaster.

The beginning of Ariel's liberation from the context of Próspero's study to a vaster horizon takes place through the schoolmaster's wishful thinking. Like the transference of Renan's Ariel to a dimension presumably outside the play, Rodó's Ariel launches into an ideological beyond. Toward the end of his farewell address, Próspero says: "Yo quiero que la imagen leve y graciosa de este bronce se imprima desde ahora en la más segura intimidad de vuestro espíritu" (p. 149). Expressing a desire to indoctrinate his students ideologically, to fashion their *reino interior*, Próspero uses Ariel as an interpellating trope with which he hopes to disseminate his perception of the statue's cultural significance. The most obvious textual device that allows Rodó to engage the attention of a broad audience is the use of the indexical, "vosotros." The elasticity of this subject pronoun incorporates the students in Próspero's study as well as the "juventud de América" to whom Rodó dedicates the essay.

In the final words of his speech, the schoolmaster envisions a wider semantic horizon for the statue. "Yo suelo embriagarme," Próspero concludes, "con el sueño del día en que las cosas reales harán pensar que la Cordillera que se yergue sobre el suelo de América ha sido tallada para ser el pedestal definitivo de esta estatua, para ser el ara inmutable de su veneración" [I am wont to inebriate myself with the dream of the day when real things will oblige us to think that the Mountain Chain that lies on America's soil has been carved to be the statue's definitive pedestal, in order to be the immutable altar of its veneration] (p. 151). In his dream, Próspero fetishizes Ariel by insisting upon a new ritualized meaning for the bronze statue. The enlargement of the statue from a literary and rhetorical to a topographical figure represents the transcendence from ideological meaning in the essay to a material object concretized ideally beyond the text's writing space.

Language (the word) is made land. After the speech, the bronze figure compounds Próspero's religious imagery of spiritual transcendence by taking on a life of its own. The following scene effectively recalls the Pentecost:

Era la última hora de la tarde. Un rayo del moribundo sol atravesaba la estancia, en medio de discreta penumbra, y tocando la frente de bronce de la estatua, parecía animar en los altivos ojos de Ariel la chispa inquieta de vida. Prolongándose luego, el rayo hacía pensar en una larga mirada que el genio, prisionero en el bronce, enviase sobre el grupo juvenil que se alejaba. (p. 153)

[It was the afternoon's final hour. A ray from the fading sun penetrated the room, through a faint penumbra, and touching the statue's bronze forehead, seemed to animate the restless spark of life in Ariel's lofty eyes. Further prolonged, the ray made one think of a long gaze that the spirit, imprisoned in the bronze, extended over the young group that was leaving.]

The independent life that Ariel displays in this closing scene – independent, moreover, because it occurs after Próspero's speech – distances the bronze statue from the schoolmaster who first invoked its cultural significance. In the tradition of the other Ariels that preceded it, Rodó's leaves its master and is transported into another dimension. This time, Ariel enters a domain fully prescribed by the schoolmaster. It takes leave of the written text to enter the fray of the overtly political and unstable discourses that inform an imagined Spanish American space.

The promotion of an icon

In this section, I trace the process of naturalization by which Rodó's essay became a Spanish American cultural icon. At one point toward the end of Próspero's speech, the schoolmaster proclaims that Ariel will prevail in its perpetual struggle with Calibán: "Vencido una y mil veces por la indomable rebelión de Calibán, Ariel resurge inmortalmente, Ariel recobra su juventud y su hermosura, y acude ágil, como al mandato de Próspero, al llamado de cuantos le aman e invocan en la realidad" [Vanquished once and a thousand times by Caliban's indomitable rebelliousness, Ariel reemerges immortal, Ariel recuperates youth and beauty, and nimbly attends, as if at Prospero's command, at the call of all those who love and invoke the genie in reality] (p. 149). Próspero, a character inside the text, proclaims the perpetual recuperability of the bronze figure not just by the students gathered around the schoolmaster but also by those outside the text who invoke it. These words have been prophetic for the essay's subsequent status in Spanish American letters. Glancing at some of the titles of the critical writings on *Ariel*, one notices that there are continuous attempts to fetishize the essay and José Enrique Rodó's figure in order to guarantee their privileged positions.[4] Even the most comprehensive study so far on Rodó's life and writings – Rodríguez Monegal 's edition of Rodó's complete works – is interspersed with the critic's attempts to defend Rodó's legacy and reputation by arguing or restating Rodó's position even against the Uruguayan's contemporaries; Rodríguez Monegal prefaces and interprets some of Rodó's correspondence in ways that are meant to attenuate or erase any aspersions cast on Rodó's character and his work. Evidently, there is more at stake in the oblivion or decanonization of *Ariel* than the simple idealization of a bronze statue. Hernán Vidal writes that "la canonización y administración burocrática de la literatura implican que la producción de significaciones para su interpretación son un foco de intensa lucha ideológica" [the canonization and bureaucratic administration of literature imply that the production of meanings for their interpretation are a focal point of intense ideological struggle] (p. 3). And when this ideological struggle is couched in terms of literature that should or should not belong to the national patrimony, it is even more intense. In order to specify the nature of this struggle – and simultaneously indicate that we should not imagine that the critics who reviewed Rodó's works formed a hegemonic group of like-minded intellectuals – I also examine the competition between the Uruguayan intellectual and Darío to champion their respective versions of an ideal, Spanish American literary expression.

Within a relatively brief period of time, Rodó was able to pose and answer for himself the question of his essay's success. In a letter to Enrique José Varona, the Cuban philosopher (Montevideo, May 7, 1900), Rodó asks: "¿Merece ser *Ariel* una bandera para la juventud intelectual americana?" [Does *Ariel* deserve to be a flag for the intellectual youth of America?] (*Obras completas*, p. 1331). About seven years later, in a letter to the Spanish historian Rafael Altamira (Montevideo, January 29, 1908), Rodó refers to the extraordinary popularity of his essay using the same analogy that he had used before to describe *Ariel*'s symbolism: "Han llegado a ser ["aquellas pobres páginas mías"] *una bandera*; y esto – por motivos superiores a la pura vanidad literaria – colma mis ambiciones de escritor" [They have come to be [those poor pages of mine] *a flag*; and this – through motives superior to pure literary vanity – is the culmination of my ambitions as writer] (p. 1363; emphasis added). This success was not as smooth as it might sound, however. A common explanation for *Ariel*'s success is its timing. According to Gordon Brotherston, for example, the essay's publication, two years after Spain lost its overseas colonies, meant that the text was certain to be read as a manifesto (see Brotherston, *Ariel*, p. 12). Nevertheless, the essay's social signification has a wider sociosemantic horizon than that indicated by this emblematic date. The Spanish Americanism for which the essay became famous is a concept that Rodó successfully negotiated in the literary market against a *modernista* aesthetics which, despite his arguments to the contrary, he also practiced in his writings. Also, more than in any of Rodó's writings, this complicated stance is visible in "Rubén Darío" (1899), a review article that rhetorically sets the stage for *Ariel*'s definition of a Spanish American cultural identity.

In Chapter 2 we noted Diana Sorensen Goodrich's observation that around the time of *Azul*'s publication poets had been turning to wealthy friends in order to finance their books and that these books, more often than not, were given away as gifts. Although this observation may be true, the practice of bestowing books on "literary friends" was not devoid of commercial motives.[5] The letters Rodó enclosed with copies of the first edition of *Ariel* that he sent to his literary friends and acquaintances reveal that these "gifts" were not pure acts of generosity but were also subject to the laws of the only intellectual circuit and commercial market available for literature – the ones provided by critics and intellectuals who had access to the media in their respective countries. Rodó was scrupulous in recording his correspondence. Rodríguez Monegal mentions that "para fiscalizar mejor tan nutrida correspondencia – que implicaba no sólo el envío de cartas, sino también la comunicación de trabajos y libros – Rodó llevaba dos registros: uno para la correspondencia enviada y recibida; otro para los impresos. En su minuciosidad, registraba hasta las dedicatorias" [in order to account better for so well fed a correspondence – which included not only outgoing letters, but also news of works and books – Rodó carried two registers: one for sent and received correspondence; another for printed matter. In his thoroughness, he kept track of even the dedications] (pp. 1319–20). For authors on both sides of the Atlantic, this correspondence offered the important mutual advantage of facilitating the dissemination of their works among the Spanish-speaking nations. Literary reviews and the correspondence that was associated with them were valued instruments for broadening a text's success. The Spanish American literary production was as dependent on Spanish literary critics as Peninsular literary works were on Spanish American critical receptions. Theoretically, at least, the political economy of literature ensured an equality of access to a pan-Hispanic reading public. This tacit recognition of a potentially wide readership determined to a great extent the formulaic character and collusive tone of the correspondence.

In the letters that he enclosed with complimentary copies of *Ariel*, Rodó briefly described the essay and its purpose. The following drafts and excerpts demonstrate that Rodó's foremost interest lay in communicating and promoting his essay's political message to an extensive audience. Referring to *Ariel* as a manifesto for the youth of America, Rodó tells the Uruguayan writer and politician, Pedro Cosio (Montevideo, February 8, 1900):

Al enviarle mi nueva obra – que espero lea usted con la atención que el tema merece, aunque el desempeño sea inferior – le pido que si tiene algún rato para dedicarlo a la holganza, escriba sobre el mismo tema, exponiendo lo que sugiera en usted la lectura de ese manifiesto dirigido a la juventud americana. Deseo que mis ideas se propaguen y que los que pueden ser sus defensores no permanezcan en silencio. Si es que escribe algo, envíelo a *La Tribuna*, donde sé que Ferreira se lo publicará con grande agrado. (*Obras completas*, p. 1370)

[On sending you my new work – which I hope you read with the attention that the theme merits, although the execution may be inferior – I ask if you have a little while to devote to leisure, that you write on the same theme, expounding on what the reading of this manifesto addressed to the American youth may suggest to you. I wish my ideas to be propagated and that those who can be their defenders not remain in silence. If you do decide to write something, send it to *La Tribuna*, where I know that Ferreira will publish it for you with great pleasure.]

In a gesture reminiscent of the effective balance of power between Prospero's books and Ariel's action in *The Tempest*, Rodó suggests that reading ought to be complemented by action. In this case, should Cosio choose to comment on the essay – the kind of "action" to which Rodó alludes – the benefit would be mutual: the recognition of both men by a select reading public. It is important to recognize that this kind of advertising marks the initial transaction through which the literary work enters the marketplace. In the letter he attached to Antonio Rubió y Lluch's complimentary copy of *Ariel* (Montevideo, March 20, 1900), Rodó once more promotes his essay as a work of action. He explains to the Catalonian intellectual his interest in seeking a certain kind of assessment of his work by Spanish critics:

Tengo verdadero interés en que ese libro se lea, porque, si el desempeño no es enteramente malo, creo que él puede hacer algún bien y sugerir ideas y sentimientos fecundos. Mi más vehemente aspiración sería que la crítica española le comentase y reconociera la buena voluntad en que se inspira, aunque juzgase con justa severidad su envoltura literaria. (p. 1329)

[I have real interest in that that book be read, because, if the execution is not entirely bad, I believe that it can do some good and suggest rich ideas and sentiments. My most vehement aspiration would be for Spanish criticism to comment on it and to recognize the good will in which it is inspired, although it might judge its literary wrapping with just severity.]

Aware of the shortcomings of the essay's literary presentation, a formula couched in modesty, Rodó expresses the desire that Spanish critics look kindly on his good intentions. He requests, in other words, that his political strategies and arguments be privileged over the literary aspects ("el desempeño") of the text. By seeking the separation of the essay's style from its supposedly straightforward political message, Rodó prescribes a reading for *Ariel* that anticipates much of the subsequent criticism on the text. Yet, this separation is not absolute but rhetorical. In his letter to Enrique José Varona, Rodó admits that his propaganda, his "buena voluntad," is not enough to guarantee the success of his work (Montevideo, May 7, 1900), and, in order to win over the Cuban philosopher's good will, he invites him to participate, through another kind of response to Rodó's call to action, in the essay's plot:

¿Merece ser Ariel una bandera para la juventud intelectual americana? Tal es mi duda que me siento inclinado a resolver negativamente, teniendo en cuenta que no basta la bondad de las ideas para el prestigio de una obra escrita, cuando le falta la autoridad de un nombre esclarecido y el encanto avasallador de la forma. Por eso anhelo que otros tomen a su cargo la propaganda que yo sólo me he atrevido a iniciar, y sería grande mi satisfacción si usted hablase a la juventud en el sentido en que yo he osado hablarle. Usted puede ser, en realidad, el *Próspero* de mi libro. Los discípulos nos agrupamos alrededor de usted para escucharle como los discípulos de Próspero. (p. 1331)

[Does Ariel deserve to be a flag for the American intellectual youth? Such is my doubt that I feel inclined to resolve it negatively, keeping in mind that the kindliness of ideas is not enough for the prestige of a written work, when it is missing the authority of an illustrious name and the engaging charm of form. For that reason I yearn for others to take charge of the propaganda that I alone have dared to initiate, and my satisfaction would be great if you spoke to the youth in the sense that I have ventured to speak to it. You can be, in reality, my book's Próspero. We disciples gather around you to listen to you like Próspero's disciples.]

Although he advises Varona to take up his cause – that is, his "propaganda" or political message – Rodó pays homage to the philosopher by identifying him with Próspero in order to convince the latter to promote the text. Clearly, these words contain an ulterior motive. In the same way that Rodó uses Próspero's speech to communicate and mediate the bronze figure's cultural meaning in *Ariel*, he eulogizes Varona as a protagonist only as far as the philosopher's protagonism is able to mediate and advocate *Ariel* as an icon.

Another illustration of Rodó's greater interest in communicating a political message than an art form are the circumstances of the correspondence he maintained with Miguel de Unamuno.[6] In his review of the essay, Unamuno writes to Rodó saying that the essay was "profundamente latina" [profoundly Latin] (p. 1376). Nevertheless, the Spanish intellectual also likened Rodó to many Spanish American artists of the period who, according to Unamuno, were unduly influenced by French culture. Eventually, as Rodríguez Monegal reports, Unamuno gave a lukewarm critique of the essay in *La Lectura*. His opinions coincide with the reservations he expressed to Leopoldo Alas about the essay, reservations which he attenuated in his correspondence with Rodó.[7] But despite Unamuno's views, Rodó's reply (Montevideo, February 25, 1901) reveals his satisfaction that Unamuno's published opinion of the essay facilitated the spread of *Ariel*'s "propaganda":

Acaba de llegar a mis manos *La Lectura*, en cuyas páginas veo el hermoso artículo que usted consagra al movimiento literario hispanoamericano y en el que tiene para mi *Ariel* frases tan benévolas como dictadas por su amistosa generosidad. Ya conocía por las cartas de usted su opinión sobre mi pobre libro; pero esta nueva manifestación de su juicio me impresiona muy gratamente porque contribuye, con la eficacia y autoridad de su palabra, a la propaganda de "Ariel." (1383)

[*La Lectura*, in whose pages I see the fine article that you devote to the Hispano-American literary movement and in which you have for my *Ariel* phrases as benevolent as they are dictated by your friendly generosity, has just gotten into my hands. I already knew about your opinion of my poor book from your letters, but this new manifestation of your judgment impresses me very nicely because it contributes, with your word's effectiveness and authority, to the propaganda of "Ariel."]

The assumption here is that unlike literature, politics and propaganda are fully transparent discourses. Rodó's preference for the political role of his work over its formal attributes is an important part of a literary politics through which his essay becomes identified with a Spanish American utopia.

The correspondent with whom Rodó is most able to establish a constructive rapport on transnational Hispanism is Leopoldo Alas (Clarín). The correspondence that Rodó and Alas maintained (1896–1900) is a study in the subtleties and limits of what Rodríguez Monegal terms a "política literaria" (see pp. 1322–8). Some of Alas's letters, with their expressions of respect and praise for the Uruguayan critic, were published in the *Revista Nacional de Literatura y Ciencias Sociales*, a biweekly review that Rodó helped to found in Montevideo in 1895. Alas is the first and most influential Spanish critic to point out the value of Rodó's criticism and intellect for the future cultural and even economic unification of Spain and Spanish America. In Barcelona's *La Saeta* (February 25, 1897), Alas calls attention to Rodó in the following manner:

[Rodó] es un crítico de cuerpo entero, que no está vinculado con ninguna de estas pestes pegajosas que tantos y tantos escritores jóvenes americanos llevan de París a su tierra. El Sr. Rodó reconoce que el jugo de las letras hispanoamericanas debe tomarse de la tradición española. . . . Críticos como el Sr. Rodó pueden hacer mucho en América, por la sincera unión moral e intelectual de España y las repúblicas hispanoamericanas; unión que podría preparar lazos políticos y económicos futuros, de los que a mi ver, ya tiene sentadas las premisas la historia, y que serán la consecuencia que saque el porvenir. (p. 1323)

[[Rodó] is a critic through and through, who is not linked to any of these contagious plagues that so very many young American writers take from Paris to their lands. Mr. Rodó recognizes that the essence of Hispano-American letters must be taken from Spanish tradition. . . . Critics like Mr. Rodó can do much in America, for the sincere moral and intellectual union of Spain and the Spanish American republics; a union that could prepare future political and economic ties, for which in my opinion, history already has its foundations laid and that will be the outcome that the future draws forth.]

Such an assessment of Rodó's role in fact weakens Rodríguez Monegal's assertion that it was with *Ariel* that America became the principal theme in Rodó's writings (p. 90). Responding to Alas's review, Rodó wholeheartedly agrees with the Spanish critic in the draft of a letter dated June 30, 1897:

Bien ha interpretado Vd. uno de los sentimientos en mí más intensos y poderosos, cuando, en las líneas que me consagra en un periódico de Barcelona, me presenta como partidario de la unión estrechísima de España y América. A contribuir a la medida de mis fuerzas a tan fecunda unión, he dedicado y me propongo dedicar en lo futuro muchos de los afanes de mi labor literaria. (p. 1323)

[Well have you interpreted one of the most intense and powerful sentiments in me, when, in the lines that you devote to me in a Barcelona newspaper, you present me as in favor of the closest union between Spain and America. To contribute to the measure of my strength to so fertile a union, have I devoted and propose to devote in the future many of the urges in my literary work.]

Literature is the means by which the union is to be sealed. In a subsequent letter to Alas (Montevideo, September 5, 1897), Rodó writes: "Y yo creo que en el arte, en la literatura, es donde más eficazmente se puede trabajar para estrechar los lazos de nuestra grande y definitiva reconciliación" [And I believe that in art, in literature, is where one can work most effectively to tighten the bonds of our great and definitive reconciliation closer] (p. 1326). Both critics have a common cultural agenda. Consequently, it is no surprise that in his review of *Ariel*, Alas praises Rodó for asking Spanish Americans to be "lo que son, . . . es decir, españoles, hijos de la vida clásica y de la vida cristiana" [what they are, . . . that is, Spaniards, the sons of classical and christian life] (Rodó, *Ariel*, p. 22). In the same review – which was originally printed in Madrid's *El Imparcial* (April 23, 1900) and, incidentally, has been inserted as a prologue to the Espasa-Calpe editions of *Ariel* – Alas declares his own concurring stance: "En esto de la unión, con toda clase de lazos, entre españoles peninsulares y españoles americanos, soy radical" [In this business of union, with all sorts of ties, among Peninsular Spaniards and American Spaniards, I am radical] (p. 11). Rodó and Alas held the same opinion about the future of Spanish America's relationship with Spain; but what Rodó emphasizes in his agenda for cultural reunion are the terms of difference that he attempts to outline between his conception of Spanish America and the one invoked by the competing aesthetics of Darío's *modernismo*. Let us turn our attention to this competition and see how it influenced critical assessments of Rodó's work.

Rodó and Darío: Toward a Spanish American aesthetic

To offer a fuller assessment of *Ariel*'s appeal throughout the Spanish-speaking world, it will be necessary to highlight the nature of Rodó's competition with Darío. The schism that the Uruguayan critic attempts to create between his conception of a Spanish American identity and the *modernistas*' version of it resembles the split that Juan Valera outlines in his critical review of *Azul* (Valera, *Obras completas 3*, pp. 289–93).[8] Even though he suggests that Nicaraguan letters are in a period of gestation, Valera forecloses the possibility of Darío's protagonism in any literary movement:

Si se me preguntase qué enseña su libro de usted y de qué trata, respondería yo sin vacilar: *no enseña nada, y trata de nada y de todo.* Es obra de artista, obra de pasatiempo, de mera imaginación. ¿Qué enseña o de qué trata un dije, un camafeo, un esmalte, una pintura o una linda copa esculpida? (p. 292; emphasis added)

[If I were asked what your book teaches and what it concerns, I would respond unhesitatingly: *it teaches nothing, and concerns nothing and everything.* It's an artist's work, a work of leisure, of mere imagination. What does a trinket, a cameo, an enamelling, a painting or a pretty sculpted cup teach or concern?]

As far as Valera is concerned, meaning in Darío's poetry is made to fall back on itself, to become entirely self-referential in a politically damaging version of art for art's sake that confines the poet to the production of form without transcendent meaning. Rodó echoes this critique by characterizing *modernismo* as superficial and trivial. However, as a critic of Darío's work, what Rodó attempts to do is to insert meaning into what Valera terms Darío's use of "signos hueros" [empty signs] (p. 292) and thus render the poet's work

accessible to a wider audience. In "Rubén Darío," Rodó deplores –
like Darío in "Palabras liminares," by the way – the circumstances
that indefinitely delay a truly free and autonomous artistic expression (p. 169). According to him, the delay results from the futile
preoccupation with an "americanismo en los accesorios"
[Americanism in accessories] (p. 169). But although Rodó readily
identifies this Americanism, he is also quick to distance the poet
from any form of leadership. In a strategy that seeks to eliminate
the competition, Rodó argues that Darío's poetry precludes him as
a leader of any autochthonous literary movement: "Tal inclinación
[el instinto del lujo . . . material y del espíritu], entre epicúrea y
platónica, a lo Renacimiento florentino, no sería encomiable como
modelo de una escuela, pero es perfectamente tolerable como
signo de una elegida individualidad" [Such a leaning [the instinct
for luxury . . . material and spiritual], between Epicurean and
Platonic, in a Florentine Renaissance style, would not be laudable
as the model for a school, but is perfectly tolerable as a sign of a
select individuality] (p. 172). In "Palabras liminares" we saw that
Darío purported to have his own inimitable style. Rodó, in the
quote above, cleverly agrees with Darío except that he considers the
poet's style too idiosyncratic to be of collective inspiration and use.

Darío also had his methods for competing with Rodó. For the
second edition of *Prosas profanas* (1901), Darío's publishers
inserted an edited version of Rodó's essay, unsigned, as the prologue. Both Darío and his publishers blamed one another for the
"mistake" (*Obras completas*, p. 1366). Sylvia Molloy comments on
this incident in her article, "Ser/Decir: Tácticas de un autorretrato":

En primer lugar, [Darío] se venga del crítico uruguayo que entre los
elogios le opone reparos, reduciéndole al anonimato, quitándole
autoridad. En segundo lugar, aprovecha el texto *pro domo sua*, borra o
disminuye las reticencias de Rodó asimilándose un estudio sin firma
que al figurar como prefacio – autorizado por Darío – no puede verse
sino como positivo. (p. 189)

[In the first place, [Darío] avenges the Uruguayan critic who between
eulogies makes objections, reducing him to anonymity, taking away
his authority. In the second place, he takes advantage of the text *pro*

domo sua, erases or diminishes Rodó's reticence by assimilating a study that upon appearing as a preface – authorized by Darío – cannot be seen but positively.]

In the same article, Molloy not only points out the competitive spirit of Rodó's "Rubén Darío" but goes on to read Darío's "Yo era aquél . . .", the first poem in *Cantos de vida y esperanza,* as the poet's response to Rodó's critique (pp. 188–9).

Despite these competitive strategies, it is still difficult to maintain that Rodó and Darío were so radically different in their approaches to representing Spanish American culture. As we have seen, *modernismo*'s subversiveness is represented by the same feature that the *antimodernistas* used to characterize poetry at the turn of the century: a superficiality instituted by a preoccupation with the signifier. Because they reduce the latter to a "literariness," to a literary language that does not insist upon the necessity of a meaning codified by European historiography, the "isolation" and sculpting of the signifier constitute the greatest threat to the uninterrupted continuity of European culture. Darío, for example, reduces Spanish artistic contributions to a range of options among which he has the power to choose. In "Palabras liminares," he describes his homage to Spanish literary tradition as if he were being conducted at his own leisure through a museum exhibition:

El abuelo español de barba blanca me señala una serie de retratos ilustres: "Este, me dice, es el gran don Miguel de Cervantes Saavedra, genio y manco; éste es Lope de Vega, éste, Garcilaso, éste Quintana." Yo le pregunto por el noble Gracián, por Teresa la Santa, por el bravo Góngora y el más fuerte de todos, don Francisco de Quevedo y Villegas. Después exclamo: "¡Shakespeare! ¡Dante! ¡Hugo . . .! (Y en mi interior: ¡Verlaine . . .!)." (*Prosas profanas,* p. 10)

[The white-bearded Spanish grandfather points out a series of illustrious portraits to me: "This one," he tells me, "is the great don Miguel Cervantes Saavedra, a genius and one-armed; this is Lope de Vega, this one, Garcilaso, this one Quintana." I ask him for noble Gracián, for Teresa the Saint, for good Góngora and the strongest of all, don Francisco de Quevedo y Villegas. Afterward I exclaim: "Shakespeare! Dante! Hugo . . .! (And inside me: Verlaine . . .!)."]

Later, in "Dilucidaciones," Darío unequivocally states his position:

El predominio en España de esa especie de retórica, aun persistente en señalados reductos, es lo que combatimos los que luchamos por nuestros ideales en nombre de la amplitud de la cultura y de la libertad.

No es, como lo sospechan algunos profesores o cronistas, la importación de otra retórica, de otro *poncif,* con nuevos preceptos, con nuevo encasillado, con nuevos códigos. Y, ante todo, ¿se trata de una cuestión de formas? No. Se trata, ante todo, de una cuestión de ideas. (p. 8)

[The predominance in Spain of that kind of rhetoric, still persistent in distinguished redoubts, is what we combat, those of us who struggle for our ideas in the name of the fullness of culture and liberty.

It is not, as some professors and columnists suspect, the importation of another rhetoric, of another *cliché,* with new precepts, a new grid, new codes. And, first and foremost, is it about a question of form? No. It is about, first and foremost, a question of ideas.]

Like Martí and others, Darío realizes that the Spanish literary tradition, similar to that of other nations, can be converted into use value, into objects of consumption in a literary market. Both Darío and Rodó consciously sifted and appropriated those European discourses that suited their cultural agendas. And it is in the belief that these practices were rooted in "una cuestión de ideas" that the two literary figures coincide substantially.

Darío's description of the liberation of Spanish American letters as an issue of ideas and not of form concurs with Rodó's certainty that both men are in essence ideologically compatible ("Rubén Darío," *Obras completas,* p. 171). Monguió writes that "Rodó veía en el Darío de *Prosas profanas . . .* un hermano en la labor de hacer de América otra Europa, de la cultura americana una cultura parigual de la europea" [Rodó saw in the Darío of *Prosas profanas . . .* a brother in the labor of making America another Europe, of American culture a culture on par with Europe's] ("De la problemática del modernismo: La crítica y el 'cosmopolitismo,'" p. 259). In "Rubén Darío," this compatibility appears in Rodó's ironic or at least ambivalent critique of *modernismo.* Almost as if he were supplementing Darío's works by describing at length the referents to which the Nicaraguan only alludes, Rodó makes critical use of the images that the poet invokes in *Prosas profanas.* He employs his prose to account for and connect the multiplicity of cultural references in Darío's texts. For example, Rodó rerepresents Darío's poem "Era un aire suave . . ." in all its dramatic fullness. He extends an invitation to his readers in which they delight not only in Darío's imagination but also in the precision with which Rodó is able to dramatize and, more significantly, to compete with and even exceed Darío's poetry:

Imaginaos un escenario que parezca compuesto con figuras de algún sutil miniaturista del siglo XVIII. Una noche de fiesta. Un menudo castillo de Le Nôtre, en el que lo exquisito de la decoración resalta sobre una Arcadia de parques. Los jardines, celados por estatuas de dioses humanizados y mundanos, no son sino salones. Los salones, traspasados por los dardos de los candelabros, arden como pastillas de quemar que se consumen. Un mismo tono, delicado y altivo, femenil y alegre, de la Grecia, triunfa por todas partes, en el gusto de la ornamentación, en los tintes claros de las telas, en las alegorías pastorales de los tapices, en las curvas femeninas de las molduras . . . Las Horas danzan fiestas. (p.175)

[Imagine a scenario that may appear composed of figures from some subtle eighteenth-century miniaturist. A gala night. A tiny Le Nôtre chateau, in which the decoration's exquisiteness stands out over an Arcadia of parks. The gardens, watched closely by statues of humanized and earthly gods, are but salons. The salons, pierced by the chandeliers' darts, glow like burning tablets that are consumed. A single tone, delicate and haughty, feminine and gay, of Greece, triumphs everywhere, in the taste of the décor, in the fabrics' light shades, in the tapestries' pastoral allegories, in the mouldings' feminine curves . . . The Hours dance the night away.]

Does this prose criticize Darío's poetry for its spiritual and material "lujo" (p. 172), or does it assume the poet's style? In the struggle between two opposing views of artistic expression, the terms of difference have been eroded. Where both discourses meet, the exchange is as denunciatory as it is adulatory. The most definitive argument that Rodó can give for the difference between his and Darío's aesthetics is the ambiguous and frequently debated statement that Rodó makes toward the end of his review of Darío's work: "Yo soy un *modernista* también" [I too am a *modernista*] (p. 191).

For Rodríguez Monegal, this statement represents Rodó's admission that he had been taken in by Darío's aesthetics. According to Monegal, it may have been the reason for the break in the correspondence between Alas and Rodó around this time (p. 1327). Nonetheless, the differences between Rodó's and Darío's view of the status of art in Spanish America may never have been as significant as Rodríguez Monegal indicates. In "Rubén Darío," Rodó explains the reason why he also sees himself as a *modernista*:

Yo pertenezco con toda mi alma a la gran reacción que da carácter y sentido a la evolución del pensamiento en las postrimerías de este siglo; a la reacción que, partiendo del naturalismo literario y del positivismo filosófico, los conduce sin desvirtuarlos en lo que tienen de fecundos, a disolverse en concepciones más altas. Y no hay duda de que la obra de Rubén Darío responde, como una de tantas manifestaciones, a ese sentido superior. (p. 191)

[I belong with all my soul to the great reaction that gives character and meaning to the evolution of thought at the end of this century; to the reaction that, starting off from literary naturalism and philosophical positivism, leads them without adulterating them in what they possess of fruitfulness, to be dissolved into higher conceptions. And there is no doubt that Rubén Darío responds, as one of so many manifestations, to this higher meaning.]

In this excerpt, Rodó appears to argue that the connection between his and Darío's aesthetics falls into a loosely defined spirit of the times. But the bond is even closer than these words might first suggest. Rodó writes of his intellectual relationship with Darío: "Yo tengo la seguridad de que, ahondando un poco más bajo nuestros *pensares*, nos reconoceríamos como buenos camaradas de ideas" [I have the assurance that, investigating a little more below our *modes of thought*, we would recognize each other as good comrades in ideas] (p. 191). On what should this friendship be based if not on the common struggle for an autonomous, Spanish American voice? In 1899 – the year after Spain's defeat in the Spanish-American War – when Darío was traveling to Spain, Rodó depicts the poet's reception for his readers: "El poeta viaja ahora, rumbo a España. Encontrará un gran silencio y un dolorido estupor. . . . Llegue allí el poeta llevando buenos anuncios para el florecer del espíritu en el habla común, que es el arca santa de la raza" [The poet travels now, on the road to Spain. He will encounter a great silence and a painful stupor. . . . May the poet arrive there bearing good news for the flowering of the spirit through common speech, which is the *raza*'s holy ark] (p. 191).

Undoubtedly, the most important common denominator for both Spanish American writers is their complementary constructions of the *modernista reino interior*. I noted in Chapter 2 how Darío perceived this interior space as the site of an artistic creativity removed from the socioeconomic contingencies of the market. Rodó, to judge by his skillful use of the political economy that supported his literary production, was more successful at promoting a specific reading of *Ariel* in the literary canon as well as in the marketplace. Nevertheless, for some critics – like Gorton Brotherston – Rodó's recourse to the celebration of a *reino interior* in order to express his political message resulted in an unfortunate "confusion" and "indecision" for his agenda. Brotherston writes:

Rodó suggests that man's highest faculty is an aesthetic one, that morality is dependent in the last resort on beauty; . . . and he assumes simultaneously that beauty is not the property of the majority but the preserve of a select minority. . . . With this he comes close to sympathizing with the attitudes of his contemporaries the *modernistas*. (p. 7)

Brotherston maintains the traditional separation between Rodó's work and that of the *modernistas*, for, according to him, "much of the *modernista* movement was nothing more than the décadence and art for art's sake of the French Parnassians and Symbolists" (p. 7). Rodó, however, is conscious of the limits of the *reino interior*. His reference to the presence of this space in Darío not only shows the extent to which he was aware of the margins of the *modernista* discourse but also indicates the manner by which he is able to appropriate and elaborate a more politicized version of the same discourse. "Su 'alcázar interior,'" Rodó writes, " – ese de que él nos habla con frecuencia – permanece amorosamente protegido por la soledad frente a la vida mercantil y tumultuosa de nuestras sociedades, y sólo se abre el *sésamo* de los que piensan, y de los que sueñan" [His "internal palace – that one about which he frequently speaks to us – remains affectionately protected by solitude in the face of the mercantile and tumultous life of our societies, and open *sesame* is only for those who think, and those who dream] ("Rubén Darío," *Obras completas*, p. 170). In this commentary, Rodó does not criticize Darío's hermetic art; rather, he emphasizes its potential comprehensibility, its communication of a message, albeit to a few. Rodó supplements Darío's *reino interior* by opening up the poet's discourse to a meaning beyond what for Brotherston is the art for art's sake of the *modernista* aesthetics of self-referentiality. By applying his usual watchwords "pensar" [think] and "sentir" [dream] to Darío's *reino interior*, Rodó, the literary critic, opens ("se abre el *sésamo*") this closed space to wider semantic horizons. Furthermore, in the most elaborated anecdote in *Ariel*, Rodó employs a *modernista* style to describe a private domain that a fictitious king kept apart for the practice of his meditation. Rodó prefaces the tale by calling it "el símbolo de lo que debe ser nuestra alma" [the symbol of what our soul ought to be] (p. 52):

Pero dentro, muy dentro aislada del alcázar ruidoso por cubiertos canales, oculta a la mirada vulgar – como la "perdida iglesia" de Uhland en lo esquivo del bosque – al cabo de ignorados senderos, una misteriosa sala se extendía, en la que a nadie era lícito poner la planta, sino al mismo rey, cuya hospitalidad se trocaba en sus umbrales en la apariencia de ascético egoísmo. Espesos muros la rodeaban. Ni un eco del bullicio exterior, una nota escapada al concierto de la Naturaleza, ni una palabra desprendida de los labios de los hombres, lograban traspasar el espesor de los sillares de pórfido y conmover una onda del aire en la prohibida estancia. . . . Graves cariátides custodiaban las puertas de marfil en la actitud del silenciario. En los testeros, esculpidas imágenes hablan de idealidad, de ensimismamiento, de reposo. (pp. 54–5)

[But within, deep within isolated from the noisy palace by covered canals, hidden from vulgar gaze – like Uhland's "lost church" in the evasiveness of the forest – at the end of unknown paths, a mysterious room stretched out, in which no one was allowed to step foot but the king himself, whose hospitality transformed itself at the threshold into the appearance of ascetic self-indulgence. Thick walls surrounded it. Not an echo from the external bustle, a wayward note from Nature's concert, not a word given off from the lips of men, managed to penetrate the thickness of the porphyr ashlars and move one waft of air in the forbidden room . . . . Grave caryatids guarded the marble doors in the quiet room's setting. On the façade, sculpted images spoke of idealness, of absorption, of repose.]

Like the poet/monk's workshop that Darío describes in "Palabras liminares," the king's private chamber is surrounded by thick walls that protect the interior from all outside disturbances. The description of this space in *Ariel* stands out amid the didactic and propagandistic prose of Rodó's essay. Its lyrical treatment of some of the common themes in *modernista* poetry makes it difficult to distinguish the style of this passage from the aesthetics from which this essay is supposed to distance itself.

Rodó claims that the recourse to the "pensar" and "sentir" of this interior realm is the sole antidote against threats not only to the integrity of the individual spirit but also to the inviolable essence of a Spanish American cultural identity. Like Darío, Rodó is cognizant of the dangers that the total, unreflexive immersion into economic life portends for the employed individual and, on a larger scale, for modern societies. According to him, the division of labor essentializes and objectifies the worker. Rodó associates this atomism with the mutilation of the spirit and hence of society. An important contributing factor to this deformation is a vocational system of education that by definition responds solely to economic demands for specialized professions. Rodó argues against the mutilation brought on by the exclusive and unbridled pursuit of material gain:

A la concepción de la vida racional que se funda en el libre y armonioso desenvolvimiento de nuestra naturaleza, e incluye, por lo tanto, entre sus fines esenciales, el que se satisface con la contemplación sentida de lo hermoso, se opone – como norma de la conducta humana – la concepción utilitaria, por la cual nuestra actividad, toda entera, se orienta en relación a la inmediata finalidad del interés. (p. 75)

[To the conception of rational life that is based on the free and harmonious development of our nature, and includes, therefore, among its essential aims, he who satisfies himself with the earnest contemplation of beauty, is opposed – as a norm of human conduct – the notion of the utilitarian, through which our activity, in its entirety, is oriented in relation to the immediate finality of gain.]

Utilitarianism, the socioeconomic counterpart of Calibán's gross materialism, is the danger that presses against the rationality of an apparently predetermined unraveling of "nuestra naturaleza" [our nature]. And, for Rodó, what community should incarnate and offer as a model this appreciation for material wealth but the United States? "Los Estados Unidos," Próspero says, "pueden ser considerados la encarnación del verbo utilitario" [The United States can be considered the incarnation of the utilitarian verb] (p. 109).[9] To resist these sieges against the integrity of personal and cultural identities, Rodó advises a return to the meditative intimacy of the *reino interior.* In the following excerpt, Próspero counsels his students (and Spanish America's youth) to adopt this resolution:

Pensar, soñar, admirar: he ahí los nombres de los sutiles visitantes de mi celda. Los antiguos los clasifican dentro de su noble inteligencia del *ocio,* que ellos tenían por el más elevado empleo de una existencia verdaderamente racional, identificándolo con la libertad del pensamiento emancipado de todo ignoble yugo. *El ocio noble era la inversión del tiempo que oponían, como expresión de la vida superior, a la actividad económica.* (pp. 56–7; emphasis added)

[Think, dream, wonder: herein lie the names of my cell's fine visitors. The ancients classify them in their noble intelligence as *leisure,* which they held as the highest use of a truly rational existence, identifying it with the freedom of thought emancipated from every detestable yoke. *Noble leisure was the investment of time that they opposed, as an expression of higher living, to economic activity.*]

In the final analysis, "ocio" or leisure provides the cure for the psychosocial maladies of the time. But by advocating leisure as the means to maintain an essential spiritual integrity ("nuestra naturaleza"), Rodó constructs and advocates a cultural identity for specific socioeconomic groups only. This political propaganda, in other words, is couched in the language of the leisure class.

Few people in Spanish America were and are able to avoid complete immersion in the activities of economic life. But by rejecting this economic dimension of daily life and, by inference, its atomistic, Calibanesque side-effects, Rodó promotes a classical, aristocratic pastime as the model for a Spanish American cultural identity. In other words, despite its critical reception as a work of action committed to the expression and dissemination of a Spanish American identity, *Ariel*'s *reino interior* appears to be as explicitly exclusive as Darío's. In an argument for a cultural identity based on the privileged activities of certain economic classes, there is no "confusion," as Brotherston would have us believe, concerning the constituencies to which Rodó directs his political and cultural agenda. That Rodó's description of the *reino interior* should complement and elaborate on Darío's – daring to propagandize what Darío "merely" poeticized – runs counter to the way in which the essay has been historicized. The terms that Rodó used to distinguish his work from Darío's cannot be the result of purely aesthetic considerations. As I have argued, Rodó's promotion of his essay to certain socioeconomic groups and through specific critical/professional practices have to a large degree determined the configurations of this difference.

5

Founding a transnational cultural literacy
The *modernista* literary reviews

Language, technology, culture

I have examined the extent to which the dissemination of *Ariel*'s political messages and cultural projects relied on a system of propaganda to actualize the essay's semantic horizons. Indeed, it may be argued that the text attained its canonized status partly because of the successful work of groups of artists and intellectuals whose correspondence, newspaper columns, and review articles provided *Ariel* with a discursive life that crossed national borders. To illustrate more fully how these groups attempted to engage and interpellate their reading constituencies, I now turn my attention to some of the *modernista* literary reviews and examine the role that these reviews and their creators played in conceptualizing, critiquing, and expressing a Spanish American cultural space. By examining the editorial remarks that introduced the inaugural number of literary reviews to readers, it is possible to glean how regional culture had been imagined. These writing spaces or – as I refer to them – manifestos represent moments in which a variety of discourses coincide. In this chapter, I explore these inscribed moments in order to illustrate how the *modernistas*' development of these new writing spaces was intimately tied to the promotion of regional cultural autonomy.

There is little doubt that journalism and the writing of articles for reviews and magazines offered the *modernistas* important areas of professional activity. According to Angel Rama, "la generación modernista fue también la brillante generación de los periodistas" [the *modernista* generation was also the brilliant generation of journalists] (*Rubén Darío y el modernismo*, p. 67). And among the various types of journalistic formats, the newspaper column provided the movement's members with an opportunity to pursue their literary vocations in creative ways. In an article that explores the role of José Martí's journalism in the development of the *modernista* movement, José Olivio Jiménez observes that "al margen (o simultáneamente) del verso y la poesía, fue la crónica periodística el género más característicamente modernista. La práctica de ese género actuó como escuela de entrenamiento para el ejercicio dinámico y brillante de la palabra a que se urgían aquellos escritores" [at the margins of (or simultaneously with) verse and poetry, the newspaper column was the most characteristically *modernista* genre. The practice of that genre acted as a training school for the dynamic and brilliant use of the word to which those writers were compelled] (p. 208). The work of Aníbal González in *La crónica modernista hispano-americana* (1983) and *Journalism and the Development of Spanish American Narrative* (1993), and Susana Rotker's *La invención de la crónica* (1992) also illustrate how the newspaper column had been characterized by the intersection and disjunctures between journalistic facticity and the flourishing of the literary in a sequential writing format. Even though this new space registered the difficulties writers experienced in adapting their vocational practices to the marketplace, it must be remembered, as Rotker argues, that the *modernistas* were at the same time intent on promoting the autonomy of literary discourse (p. 60).

Under pressing circumstances that signaled the loss of social status, these writers actively sought to empower themselves through the aesthetic elaboration of "facts." In light of their efforts to preserve the literary and, in the best of scenarios, to promote it over other competing, intellectual discourses, such as philology – González observes (*Journalism and the Development of Spanish American Narrative*, pp. 18, 85) – it is no surprise that the literary review became for the *modernistas* a writing space in which they could take their work to its furthest aesthetic and geographical extensions. Darío's *Azul*, for example, is often cited as the *chef-d'oeuvre* that launched the *modernista* movement in Spanish America; yet it must be remembered that this book is a collection of poems and stories previously published by the Chilean reviews *La Epoca, Revista de Artes y Letras*, and *La Libertad Electoral*.[1]

However, before examining some of the manifestos that launched the literary reviews, it will be necessary to look at the ideological and cultural importance that has been generally ascribed to these publications. In *Literatura y sociedad en América Latina: El modernismo*, Françoise Pérus registers the literary movement's development in direct relation to the penetration of European capitalism into Spanish America between 1880 and 1910. Because in this kind of critical approach, the reviews have too unhesitatingly been associated with economic expansion, the modernization of urban infrastructures, and the concurrent emergence of national and regional consciousness, I argue in this section of the chapter that the "progressive" technologies that provided for the dissemination of *modernista* cultural agendas were the instruments and not the agents of engagement. Because of certain propensities toward infusing the economic with subjectivity – especially in the social sciences and their related approaches to literature – this argument is not as obvious as it might first seem. Inquiring into the social specificity of those technologies should not separate so uncritically the literary movement's cultural ideology from its political economy.

The perspective that I offer here represents an effort to mitigate approaches to the contingency of nationalism and the press, such as Benedict Anderson's in *Imagined Communities*, which can sometimes overestimate the technical activity of the publishing industry because they view technology as the principal catalyst of national sentiment. Inadvertently or not, Anderson suggests that print capitalism ossifies language into more or less effective bureaucratic models of noncontestatory "print languages." This conflation of capitalism and language cannot account for representations of ideological struggles within language itself. In the second part of this chapter, I reassert (vis-à-vis Anderson's notion of community) an ideological engagement that emphasizes the desire for community and its articulation through rhetorical strategies.

As potential vehicles for a common cultural expression, the *modernista* literary reviews enjoy a uniquely powerful role in the movement's criticism. Boyd Carter, for example, claims that Mexico's *Revista Azul* was the first and foremost means of mediating and inspiring Hispano-American cultural unity:

Es lícito suponer que casi todas estas revistas, en su mayoría órganos del movimiento modernista, y también otras muchas a las que no aludimos, debían su vida a la fructífera existencia de la *Revista Azul.* Nunca antes y acaso nunca después pudo alcanzar el concepto de la unidad cultural de Hispanoamérica el alto grado de recíproca identidad que se realizó en la *Revista Azul.* Aun cuando los modernistas no quisieron encararse con los problemas fundamentales de sus países y de su época, no dejaban de tener plena conciencia de la obra literaria de sus colegas, porque colaboraron todos en las mismas revistas. (p. 356)²

[It is permissible to suppose that almost all these reviews, for the most part organs of the *modernista* movement, and many others to which we do not allude, owed their life to *Revista Azul*'s fruitful existence. Never before and perhaps never afterward could the concept of Hispano-American cultural unity attain the high degree of reciprocal identity that was realized in *Revista Azul.* Even when the *modernistas* refused to face their countries' and era's fundamental problems, they did not fail to have full awareness of their colleagues' literary work, because they all collaborated in the same reviews.]

Even though he subscribes to the escapist detachment hypothesis, Carter nonetheless claims that the *Revista Azul* represented the superlative expression of a Spanish American identity. Although Carter posits a reciprocal relationship between the review and a regional cultural expression, some critics perceive these publications as instrumental for the spread of certain ideologies of culture. Guillermo Korn notes, for instance, that "*El Cojo Ilustrado* incorpora a Venezuela – pese a todas las limitaciones coactivas en el orden político – a la renovación positivista impregnada de fe creadora en el Progreso y la Ciencia" [*El Cojo Ilustrado* incorporates Venezuela – despite all the coercive limitations in the political order – in the positivist renewal impregnated by creative faith in Progress and Science] (p. 5). Although Korn writes about the a priori existence of the Venezuelan nation, there is no doubt that in this context "nation" is a passive entity brought under the "civilizing" tutelage of the positivism espoused by the publication. In these assessments, literary reviews "imagine" Spanish America and concretize the region in their pages.

Yet, in this confluence of discourses on socioeconomic progress and cultural definition, economic expansion often becomes the privileged trope of cultural meaning. Notice in the following excerpt how Luis Monguió describes the movement's aesthetics not only in terms of intertextual models but also as if it were an imported technology:

En la segunda mitad del siglo XIX la literatura española se hallaba en un estado que no lo hacía modelo deseable. Por otra parte, los países hispanoamericanos, con sus riquezas, acaban de entrar en el campo de explotación de los grandes países industriales expansionistas de Europa, a los que los grupos detentadores del poder y de la cultura en la América española miraban como líderes de la economía, de la civilización y de la cultura, a los que era deseable igualarse. Entre tales países, Francia ofrecía culturalmente los mejores modelos y los más asequibles al espíritu hispanoamericano. De este mimetismo, unido al lirismo del escritor de la América española, nació un movimiento literario, singularmente en poesía, en el que con las nuevas ideas y a través de la asimilación de nuevos procedimientos técnicos elaborados por escuelas literarias extranjeras, se produjo una renovación ideológica y técnica en la literatura de lengua española. ("Sobre la caracterización del modernismo," p. 21)

[In the second half of the nineteenth century Spanish literature found itself in a condition that did not render it a desirable model. On the other hand, the Hispano-American countries, with their riches, recently entered the field of exploitation of Europe's great expansionist, industrial countries, toward which the unlawful holders of power and culture in Spanish America looked as leaders of the economy, of civilization, and of culture, and with which it was desirable to be on par. Among such countries, France offered culturally the best models and the most accessible ones for the Hispano-American spirit. From this mimicry, bound to the Spanish American writer's lyricism, a literary movement was born, uniquely in poetry, in which with new ideas and through the assimilation of new technical procedures elaborated by foreign literary schools, an ideological and technical renewal in Spanish-language literature was produced.]

Except for the local raw material – the unexplained "lirismo" of the Spanish American writer – the *modernista* technical expertise comes from France. Monguió's analysis implies that external agents sustain the movement, and it is not surprising, from the perspective of this dependency model, that he ultimately associates the decline in the movement's popularity with the economic, philosophical, and cultural disorder in Europe around 1914 (pp. 21–2).

In 1983, these kinds of approaches to understanding the construction of national identities through literature culminated in Benedict Anderson's seminal *Imagined Communities*. In his study, Anderson investigates the relationship between print technology and the proliferation of nation states in the last century. His principal argument is that the nation can be imagined in the act of reading because of the reciprocal and simultaneous awareness that readers have of their own collective existence. What formerly was too vast a reality to apprehend – that is, the perceived existence of all the individuals of the national community – becomes more tangible through publications and their readership. Central to the formation of "the bases for national consciousness" is Anderson's elaboration of what he calls "print-languages" (p. 47). These languages were instrumental in three ways: they generated fields of linguistic exchange that allowed for the continuous evolution and play of a standard language; once this field of exchange had been established, "print-capitalism gave a new fixity to language" (p. 47), significantly slowing the rate of change in languages until, by the seventeenth century, European languages had already attained their modern forms; and, finally, print-capitalism set up a hierarchy of languages based on their proximity to the older administrative vernaculars. In summing up his remarks regarding the importance of print-languages for the development of national consciousness, Anderson states: "It remains only to emphasize that in their origins, the fixing of print-languages and the differentiation of status between them were largely unselfconscious processes resulting from the explosive interaction between capitalism, technology and human linguistic diversity" (p. 48).

That Anderson should refer to the fixing of print-language – according to him, the very proof of the existence of a national consciousness – as an unselfconscious process reveals the difficulty that he encounters in justifying his conflation of "imagined" (a form of subliminal recognition) and "community" (a desired model of social organization). In other words, by defining the relationship he had previously drawn between capitalism, technology, and language as an "unselfconscious" process, the result of an uncontrolled, explosive interaction, Anderson contradicts his claim that the concept of the nation is what he terms "'modular,' capable of being transplanted, *with varying degrees of self-consciousness*, to a variety of social terrains" (p. 14; emphasis added). Much of the contradiction may be explained by a closer look at Anderson's use of the word "imagined" not to describe how or in what terms the community is represented through language but to emphasize by what technical means the image of the community is instantaneously conjured. Although he couches the community's awareness as "consciousness," this condition is more technological that ideological. The quantification of national consciousness leads Anderson to assert that "the newspaper reader, observing exact replicas of his own paper being consumed by his subway, barbershop, or residential neighbours, is continually reassured that the imagined world is visibly rooted in everyday life" (p. 39). The community that imagines itself along the lines of Anderson's argument does so in the absolute terms of market values.[3] And only from the perspective of these values can Anderson speak of languages and, by inference, of a national consciousness based on the potential that these languages have, as he writes, of "insisting on their own print-form" (p. 48).

That technology is able to quantify language and experience leads Anderson to speak of societies in history in the following terms: "The idea of a sociological organism moving calendrically through homogeneous, empty time is a precise analogue of the idea of nation, which also is conceived as a solid community moving steadily down (or up) history" (p. 31). This statement is characterized by a biotechnical language in which the community, like an automotive piston, is made to ascend and descend the cylinder of history. Indeed, the "explosive interaction between capitalism, technology and human linguistic diversity" that he designates as the origin of print-languages may well be the combustion for Anderson's idea of the nation. This overdetermination logically follows from his interpretation of Walter Benjamin's notion of "aura" – a term that Benjamin uses to describe the immediacy of the work of art's fetishized existence in the age of mechanical reproduction. When he explains his use of the word "simultaneity," Anderson writes:

What has come to take the place of the medieval conception of simultaneity-along-time is, to borrow again from Benjamin, an idea of "homogeneous, empty time," in which simultaneity is, as it were, transverse, cross-time, *marked not by prefiguring and fulfillment, but by temporal coincidence,* and measured by clock and calendar. (p. 30; emphasis added)

Anderson privileges immediacy over "prefiguring and fulfillment." In other words, by eliminating the trajectory of desire over time, from the moment of its arousal ("prefiguring") to that of its gratification ("fulfillment"), Anderson discards communal desire as an important politicizing and utopian force in the ideologies that inform nationalism.

An analysis that perceives national consciousness as a phenomenon accessible only through simultaneity can lead to a dangerous reductionism: the representation of this historical experience in absolutes of success or failure. With respect to administration and commerce in Spanish America, Anderson states: "The 'failure' of the Spanish-American experience to generate a permanent Spanish-America-wide nationalism reflects both the general level of development of capitalism and technology in the late eighteenth century and the 'local' backwardness of Spanish capitalism and technology in relation to the administrative stretch of the empire" (p. 63). By contrast, the American colonies to the North were more successful at realizing nationhood:

The Protestant, English-speaking creoles to the north were much more favourably suited for realizing the idea of "America" and indeed eventually succeeded in appropriating the everyday title of "Americans." The original Thirteen Colonies comprised an area smaller than Venezuela, and one third the size of Argentina. Bunched geographically together, their market-centres in Boston, New York, and Philadelphia were readily accessible to one another, and their populations were relatively tightly linked by print as well as commerce (p. 64)

As historical experiences, therefore, national movements are directly proportional to the efficiency and geographical extension of a marketplace and its attendant print-capitalism. According to this perspective, the "successful" nation relies on the absolute commensurability of national culture and geopolitical borders. In any case, Anderson's view that as a political state the United States appropriated the name "America" should not be the yardstick against which Latin America's transnational identity is measured. To support his claim that the United States realized "the idea of 'America,'" Anderson ignores the ability of Spanish colonial administrations to maintain political hegemony in Spanish America. The independence of the United States and the longevity of the Spanish Empire both represent forms of nationalism (one American and land-locked; the other European and maritime) that differ according to the value placed on geopolitical "rationality" and political rupture as defining features of the modern nation. Anderson's criteria sets Spanish American national experiences against a background of so-called economic backwardness and, by implication, of political underdevelopment. This approach uncritically identifies Latin America with that underdevelopment. A more valid comparison to make with the United States might have been the unification of Mexico, Argentina, or Brazil – large countries with regionalisms and vast natural resources that eventually became subsumed into larger nation-building projects. Anderson's comparative look at the Americas leaves no room to consider the fact that at the time of their respective independence from former colonizers the political elite both in the United States and Latin America maintained strong cultural and flourishing economic ties with Europe.

In the final analysis, to understand the politics of printed language in *modernista* literary reviews (in a less rigid manner than Anderson's notion of print language) what will be required is a conceptualization of language and transnational ideology that would not measure its ability to recruit subscribers on the basis of an infrastructure alone.

Toward a discriminating readership

Now, in order to imagine the Spanish American community through the politics (and not the bureaucratic functionalism) of language, let us turn our attention to the ways in which the creators of *modernista* literary reviews invoked a desire for that community. The inaugural statements of these reviews contain a utopian impulse, a "prefiguring and fulfillment" of Spanish American national and regional self-knowledge and a critique of the present. Their metadiscursive function – for they are texts whose object of scrutiny is writing – facilitates the examination of the political economy of writing in a manner similar to Enzensberger's study of the eulogy. A focus on the language of the periodicals' opening editorial comments permits an analysis not only of the kinds of publishing criteria and cultural agendas that their founders and editors merged and promoted but also of the type of readership they sought. The anticipatory character of these opening remarks creates new writing spaces in a textual continuity otherwise known as a literary movement. In their promotion of a particular cultural literacy, these inaugural statements may be called manifestos. "Sur le plan fonctionnel," writes Jean-Marie Gleize, "tout manifeste est une préface générale à un ensemble d'oeuvres possibles" [On the functional plane every manifesto is a general preface to an ensemble of possible works] (p. 13). In associating the manifesto's anticipated audience with texts written in brochures, journals, or reviews (p. 3), Claude Abastado argues that the manifesto "met en forme . . . la pensée latente d'un public virtuel" [gives form to . . . the latent thought of a virtual public] (p. 8).[4] Aníbal González's study of the *modernista* newspaper column suggests a useful way to think about writing as a progression of texts that extends indefinitely into the future:

La escritura de la crónica no sólo presupone una concepción lineal y progresiva del tiempo . . . sino que se ocupa de realizar un *análisis* del devenir: la crónica subdivide la progresión temporal en una multitud de instantes discretos, en una pululación de eventos que es necesario historiar, fijar dentro de una trama que es a la vez temporal y narrativa. (*La crónica modernista hispanoamericana.*, p. 73)

[The column's writing not only presupposes a linear and progressive conception of time . . . but it is concerned with achieving an *analysis* of the future: the column subdivides temporal progression into a multitude of discreet moments, into a bustle of events that it is necessary to depict, to fix within a plot that is at once temporal and narrative.]

This approach to writing derives from the association that González draws between the newspaper column's physical division of "real" time (concept) and its ability to transpose that time into a multiplicity of inscribed moments (tangible form). These theoretical definitions of attempts to inscribe the future permit me to discern the very borders of *modernista* histories of their present; they also allow for the identification of modernity with the emergence of a Spanish American transnationalism.

In some of the *modernista* reviews, this conflation of the experience of modernity and the emergence of Spanish Americanism inhabits a space of imminence and engagement that is often expressed through a subjunctive mood. According to John Lyons, "the traditional term 'subjunctive' . . . comes from the Latin translation of the Greek word for 'subordinating' and shows that for the traditional grammarian the subjunctive was the mood of subordination *par excellence*" (p. 312). This use of the subjunctive is not exactly what one might want to call, as Eagleton does, a "'bad' or premature utopianism" (p. 25). Rather, its usage activates an appeal to readers that transcends the written text as an editorial promise to historicize and thereby subordinate the future in a manner that would please the reading public. It is in this ethereal territory beyond inscription that the *modernistas*' experience of modernity as the inevitability of progress and the discursive emergence of the Spanish American community appear inextricable. In broader terms, the provisionary character of the subjunctive unfolds at the heart of political engagement and through a credible allegorization of the community or, in Althusser's language, "interpellation." Although I noted in the Introduction how Jameson's emphasis on the allegorical nature of the relation between a self-conscious collectivity and its utopia depends on such a conditionality, it is worth repeating the specific language that he uses to express these ideas:

all class consciousness of whatever type is Utopian *insofar as* it expresses the unity of a collectivity; yet it must be added that this proposition is an allegorical one. The achieved collectivity or organic group of whatever kind – oppressors fully as much as oppressed – is Utopian

not in itself, but *only insofar as* all such collectivities are themselves figures for the ultimate concrete collective life of an achieved Utopian or
classless society. (*The Political Unconscious*, p. 291; emphasis added)

Jameson's view of the allegorical relationship between a community and its utopia and Althusser's conception of the dynamics
between the subject and ideology are rendered by similar expressions. Althusser states that "the category of the subject is only con-
stitutive of all ideology *insofar as* all ideology has the function
(which defines it) of 'constituting' concrete individuals as subjects" ("Ideology and Ideological State Apparatuses," p. 171;
emphasis added). Not only do these expressions attempt to join
the particular and the universal but they do so by rendering
through language the perpetually symbolic imminence of the
community.

Some of the reviews' opening statements employ the subjunctive at the site where their founders and editors define their publications' role as the purveyors not only of self-awareness but also of
national and regional, socioeconomic progress. For example, in
their first issue (September 15, 1891), the editors of *La Habana
Literaria* fashion a review to satisfy a variety of tastes: "Es nuestro
objeto publicar una revista ilustrada, en la cual, mediante el
carácter enciclopédico que ha de distinguirla, *encuentren* satisfacción los diversos gustos y las aficiones distintas de los lectores" [It
is our object to publish an illustrated review, in which, by means of
the encyclopedic character that is to distinguish it, the readers'
sundry pleasures and individual hobbies *may find* satisfaction]
(Hernández Miyares and Zayas, p. 1; emphasis added).[5] The use of
the subjunctive here signals a gesture of engagement that goes
beyond inscription. At the same time, it posits this gesture as an
invitation to attend to its readers' desires and whims and entertain
them with hobbies – in other words, it attempts to set in motion a
specific cultural literacy. "En consecuencia," the editors continue,

la prosa y el verso se repartirán en conveniente proporción las páginas
de la revista, y en ellas se leerán junto a los artículos de amena literatura, serias e instructivas disertaciones, que sin árido tecnicismo ni
fatigosa amplitud, *den* á conocer el movimiento progresivo de las artes

y ciencias, o *expongan* los problemas de la política y los adelantos de las industrias. (p. 1; emphasis added)

[As a result, prose and verse will be conveniently apportioned in the review's pages, and in them next to articles on pleasant literature serious and instructive dissertation will be read, which, without arid jargon or tiresome broadness, *may provide* knowledge about the progressive movement of the arts and sciences, or *expound* on the problems of politics and the advances of industries.]

These instances of the subjunctive describe the review's forthcoming articles; they attempt through language to concretize the editors' future, discursive positions. Also, it is by no means coincidental that this vow to publish neatly parallels the progressive movement of the arts, science, and industry. As I show in the course of this discussion, the opening remarks of Buenos Aires' *La Biblioteca* and *Revista de América* and Caracas' *Cosmópolis* contain statements that similarly anticipate the public's desire and locate the subjunctive in a syntactical and ideological space that links readership to a regional self-awareness.

The subjunctive conditionality of *La Habana Literaria*'s inaugural address, "Al público," is also expressed as a collective emotion and attitude toward the future: the review's founders base their prospects in the market on the hope that their readers will recognize the publication's desire to please subscribers. This conception of hope is an example of the kind that informs the pan-Hispanism of "Salutación del optimista." It is not a sign of resignation in the face of insurmountable obstacles but of optimism and, as far as founders and editors were concerned, a belief in the review's potential to attract readers. In the appeal that *La Habana Literaria* makes to readers, it is on the strength of hope that the review's success lies:

Ardua y por demás erizada de dificultades, es la empresa que intentamos realizar, que siempre ha sido en nuestro país tarea ingrata y de dudoso éxito la publicación de un periódico. Sin embargo, al iniciar la de *La Habana Literaria* nos anima una halagüeña esperanza, tal vez ilusoria, nacida del aplauso dado a nuestro proyecto por benévolos amigos, pero que nos inclina a pensar que este público inteligente e ilustrado, reconociendo nuestro deseo de agradarle premiará nuestros afanes dispensando protección al nuevo periódico. (p. 1)

[Arduous and also bristling with problems, is the enterprise that we are attempting to achieve, for in our country the publication of a newspaper has always been a thankless task, of dubious success. Nevertheless, upon initiating that of *La Habana Literaria* a gratifying hope animates us, perhaps illusory, born of the applause given to our project by benevolent friends, but which makes us inclined to think that this intelligent and enlightened public, recognizing our desire to please it, will reward our urges by dispensing protection to the new newspaper.]

Far from being a weak admission of intentionality, this expression of hope is a political and marketing stance backed up by strategic planning. It grounds itself in a power relationship that in the case of *La Habana Literaria* takes the form of a magnanimous gesture of courtesy: the review's desire to please the public (a polite assertion of the publication's studied bid to create a reading constituency) will seek compensation in the public's protection (a concession of power to supposedly passive readers).[6] Hope, therefore, represents a complex rhetorical move to found a tangible community . . . one that can be confidently categorized with hindsight. For example, the October 7, 1899 edition of *Caras y Caretas* records the successful implementation of "hope." Here the editors account for their success a year after launching the first number of the review in Buenos Aires:

creamos un tipo de periódico como, después de maduro estudio de la psicología del lector bonaerense, creíamos que ensamblaría mejor en su gusto. La nota fuerte de color al frente, con una gracia cuando era posible, con un propósito de sátira moral siempre, y siempre tratando de poner en esa nota inicial de la carátula la traducción gráfica de un sentimiento público, lealmente explorado. Por algo entra así el periódico en la brega de todos por el mejoramiento de instintos y de costumbres, de cosas y de ideas. (Alberdi and Payró, p. 90)

[we created a type of newspaper that, after prudent analysis of the Buenos Aires reader's psychology, we believed would hold together best for his taste. The strong colorful note in the front, with a witty remark when possible, always with a regard to moral satire, and always

trying to present in that initial touch on the cover the graphic translation of a faithfully explored public sentiment. Hence the reason why
the newspaper thus enters everyone's struggle for the improvement of
instincts and of customs, of things and ideas.]

According to this explanation, the editors are able to assert that
the reader in Buenos Aires responds to tried and tested visual
stimuli. The psychology of the reader in turn seems to be predi-
cated on the ability of the review's creators to inculcate an appreciation for distinguishable aesthetic formulas. It is on the basis of
this appreciation that the founders and editors claim that they in
effect contributed to social improvements in Buenos Aires.

  The expression of hope and the desire to please readers, however, can sometimes lean more toward the instrumentality of the
publication's role in the public sphere. In *La Habana Literaria*,
Zayas and Hernández Miyares define their review's place in Cuban
society:

Conocidas, como son, las condiciones en que se desarrollan nuestras
empresas periodísticas, es ocioso que protestemos no ser el lucro lo
que nos mueve a publicar *La Habana Literaria*, y no faltamos a la verdad al indicar como nuestra primordial aspiración la de coadyuvar de
algún modo, y en el límite de nuestras fuerzas, al progreso intelectual
y moral del país, en cuyo progreso es innegable la eficaz participación
de la prensa, cuando para inspirar su conducta y procedimientos no
olvida la noble y levantada misión que está llamada a cumplir. (p. 2)

[Recognizing as they are, the conditions in which our journalistic
enterprises develop, it is idle for us to protest that it is not profit that
encourages us to publish *La Habana Literaria*, and we do not disrespect
truth by indicating as our primary aspiration that of facilitating in
some way, and to the limits of our strength, the country's intellectual
and moral progress, in whose advance the press' effective participation is undeniable, when in order to inspire its conduct and procedures it does not forget the noble and lofty mission that it is sum-
moned to accomplish.]

The review's role is not merely that of contributing to the public
good but, in addition, that of fulfilling certain moral responsibilities. An extreme version of this imposed instrumentality appears in
La Biblioteca's introductory statement where its founder, Paul

Groussac, indicates: "Es muy sabido que, por lo regular, la necesidad crea el instrumento: pero lo contrario acontece también, y no es raro que la presencia inesperada de un órgano nuevo determine y estimule la función" [It is well known that, regularly, necessity invents the instrument: but the opposite happens as well, and it is not unusual for the unexpected presence of a new organ to determine and stimulate the function] (p. 7). This privileging of function over necessity – an imposition of structure and order from above – captures the positivism and manipulative ideology with which Groussac and others approached the reading public and, by extension, culture.

So far, I have been concentrating on a *modernista* site of enunciation. However, as I have already pointed out in *La Habana Literaria*'s declaration of intent, the most important goal behind the formation of this site was to stimulate collective discourses of power. These discourses informed various agendas; in this study I concentrate on two that overlap in ways that refer us once more to the conflation of attempts at inscribing modernity and the emergence of a community. The first gesture toward unification in the reviews is that of an invitation that organized groups of founders and editors extend to readers; the second discourse maps this collective of like-minded writers and readers onto national and regional spaces.

According to Hernán Vidal, "la aparición en el horizonte profesional de la noción de la investigación en equipo . . . es índice de las nuevas relaciones sociales que se anuncian" [the appearance on the professional horizon of team investigation . . . is an index of new social relations that call attention to themselves] (p. 8). In Korn's description of the work of *El Cojo Ilustrado*'s editors, intellectual cooperation is expressed as a mandate: "El conjunto de personalidades disconformes emprendedores – impresores, periodistas, escritores, artistas y hombres de ciencia – que se agrupan en torno a la revista lo hacen movidos por un imperativo que a todos los domina por igual" [The collection of enterprising diverse personalities – printers, journalists, writers, artists and men of science – that come together around the review do so moved by an imperative that equally dominates all] (p. 30). The manifestos that launch the first issues of literary publications in Spanish America at the turn of the century are grounded in the ubiquitous reference to plural subject positions, to configurations of the indexical "we."[7] The text entitled "Nuestros propósitos" that inaugurated the *Revista de América*, for example, outlines a cultural agenda signed by "La Dirección" (p. 1). Similar formulations in other publications allude to the authority of this editorial body.

One of the first steps that the reviews' creators undertake toward establishing a reading constituency is to recognize a public that is as culturally literate as they are. Rhetorically, this move discursively creates an audience and market for their writing. This mutually gratifying relationship between the reviews' creators and their potential readers is adequately rendered in the advice that the first president of the Ateneo de Buenos Aires, Calixto Oyuela, offers his audience in an essay entitled "Asociaciones literarias" (December 1906):

Para que las letras puedan cultivarse dignamente en una sociedad, es ante todo necesario que exista un público que se interese por ellas, que anime y estimule al escritor con su estimación y su aplauso, y aun comprándole sus obras. Es necesario que el escritor no escriba soliloquios; que ejerza en el público una influencia eficaz y levante su eco en su corazón y su conciencia. (p. 368)

[For letters to be cultivated with dignity in a society, it is before all else necessary that there exist a public that is interested in them, that urges and stimulates the writer with its critique and its applause, even buying his works. It is necessary for the writer not to write soliloquies; for him to exercise effective influence on the public and for him to raise an echo in hearts and conscience.]

In *La Habana Literaria*'s inaugural remarks, Hernández Miyares and Zayas not only recognize their public but also esteem it as a "público ilustrado e inteligente" [enlightened and intelligent public]. By adulating the enlightenment and intelligence of their readers, the editors attempt to create an enclave in which these characteristics literally become, through language and reading, the exclusive domain of the review's contributors and readers. Oyuela suggests that this appreciation for the public is an ultimately necessary evil in order to gain its attention:

Es para mí evidente que el «oficio literario», como medio único de vida, tiene grandísimos inconvenientes, y acaba por ser contrario a la alta producción artística. Si malo es depender de un príncipe, también lo es depender del público, a cuyo nivel hay que ponerse y a quien hay que adular y se adula infinitas veces para que compre la mercadería. (p. 369)

[For me it is evident that the "literary profession," as a sole means of livlihood, has enormous inconveniences, and ends up being contrary to high artistic production. If it is bad to depend on a prince, so too is it to depend on the public, at whose level it is necessary to put oneself and whom it is necessary to adulate an infinite number of times in order for it to buy the merchandise.]

In the first issue of *La Biblioteca*, Groussac describes the context of the review's appearance in the public sphere: "Así como, desde los primeros pasos, hemos hallado una cooperación intelectual, superior en todo sentido a muchas previsiones, no es imposible que, a la larga, responda el público a nuestro llamamiento, y que encontremos, para nuestras páginas, la audiencia y el concurso merecidos" [Just as, from the first steps, we have found an intellectual collaboration, superior in every sense to all forecasts, it is not impossible that, in the long run, the public may respond to our call, and that we find, for our pages, the audience and support that are deserved] (p. 7). For Groussac, a high degree of intellectual cooperation defines both a potential readership and the editorial group itself. Like the salute and the surreptitious self-referentiality of the poetic voice in "Salutación del optimista," this act of addressing and hailing the public in laudatory terms transforms Groussac's message into a self-empowering utterance.

And like the manipulative ideology of culture that informs the *reino interior*, this editorial self-naming engenders an exclusive space from which the reviews' creators subsequently exercise power. When he argues that "a politics of difference or specificity is in the first place in the cause of sameness and universal identity" (p. 30),

Eagleton suggests that the utopian celebration of universality is in the final analysis self-promotional. Eagleton makes this claim in reference to some of the ironies in struggles against colonialism. Nevertheless, this statement, I believe, is theoretically valid for most instances of identity politics. Gleize notices the same phenomenon in the manifesto: "en droit le manifeste est à destination universelle, il suppose l'illimitation du destinaire; en fait il s'adresse à un petit peuple d'élus; il nomme restrictivement (et rend cette restriction officielle) les véritables sectateurs, le clan des grands ortodoxes: à la limite, ce qui le caractérise c'est l'autodestination" [as a rule the manifesto is meant for universal address, it supposes the limitlessness of the addressee; in fact it addresses itself to a small select community; it restrictively names (and renders that restriction official) the true separatists, the clan of great orthodox ones: at best, what characterizes it is self-referentiality] (pp. 14–15).

An example of this self-referentiality can be found in *Cosmópolis'* opening remarks, where the review's founders produce a brief drama or "Charloteo" (Coll et al.) in which they are featured as the only characters. In this metacritical play (that is both a manifesto and a self-congratulatory gesture), Pedro Coll focuses on the publication's collaborative efforts in the first line of a writing space that is intended for public viewing: "Queridos cofrades, estamos solos, nadie nos oye y podemos hablar con franqueza" [Dear brothers, we are alone, nobody hears us and we can speak frankly] (p. 1). This feigned erasure of the border between the public and the private represents a call to participate in a form of exclusivity that disguises itself as accessibility. In this inaugural issue, the founders appreciate their relationship with one another in terms of a cultural identity and familial ties mediated by a common language and literature: "Nosotros, hijos de la misma madre, permanecíamos desconocidos unos de otros pero ahora gracias a la literatura y a los periódicos que surgen en todas las Repúblicas españolas, nos saludamos como hermanos, nos conocemos y estamos alegres como en plena luna de miel" [We, children of the same mother, had remained mutual strangers but now thanks to literature and to newspapers that are emerging in all the Spanish Republics, we greet each other like siblings, we know each other and are merry as if fully on honeymoon] (p. 4). On the one hand, they base the recognition of the Spanish American community on the expansion of presses and the reciprocity of intellectual collaboration; on the other, they recognize this community by means of a "private" conversation that they consider a non-communicative series of utterances or chattering ("charloteo").

Extending membership to a particular kind of imagined community through a program of cultural literacy is evident in several reviews. In the midst of celebrating the fruition of a regional intelligentsia, there are manifestos that proclaim starkly elitist agendas. The editors of Buenos Aires' *Revista de América*, for instance, propose to "servir en el Nuevo Mundo y en la ciudad más grande y práctica de la América latina, a la aristocracia intelectual de las repúblicas de lengua española" [to serve in the New World and in the largest and most practical city in Latin America, the intellectual aristocracy of the Spanish-speaking republics] (p. 1), a group to which, by dint of their mediation as the purveyors of literature, they must also belong. Mexico's *Revista Azul* similarly conceptualized its invitation to readers in a text called "Al pie de la escalera" [At the foot of the stairwell]. In this first issue (May 6, 1894), Manuel Gutiérrez Nájera promises to cultivate a special readership. Imagining the review as a house and access to its readership as a staircase, he states, referring to the latter: "No es de mármol, pero subid. Hay flores en el corredor y alegría de buen tono en los salones" [It is not made of marble, but go up. There are flowers in the corridor and fashionable merriment in the salons] (p. 2). In the same way that Rodó asserts in *Ariel* that an acquired aesthetic experience should determine the recognition of one's class allegiance and cultural identity, those who enter the editors' (publishing) house must also acknowledge why it is necessary for him to point out these "basic" amenities. Steeped in the arts of leisure, this gentility illustrates the extent to which the community that the *Revista Azul*'s editors imagine was socioeconomically segregated. "El Arte, señores míos," continue Gutiérrez Nájera and Díaz Dufóo, "se roza con los de arriba y se codea con los de abajo . . . Porque en materia de Arte, yo no conozco más géneros que dos: el bueno y el malo. Queda el regular. Peor que el malo, créanlo ustedes" [Art, good sirs, brushes against those upstairs and elbows its way with those downstairs. Because in matters of Art, I am not acquainted with but two genres: the good and the bad. The mediocre is left. Worse than the bad one, believe it] (p. 4).

One of the most common means by which the authors of these manifestos attempt to broaden their community is the rhetorical use of theological discourses and tropes. For example, in refusing to formulate a program of action, Gutiérrez Nájera and Díaz Dufóo critique the language and practice of parliamentary government and at the same time promote the autonomy of their literary discourse. Pushing to liberate the arts, they employ a particular religious trope to negate the efficacy of parliamentary governmental procedure:

En los gobiernos parlamentarios, cada ministerio entrante presenta su programa. ¡Es de rigor! Y cada uno de esos programas, se parece a muchos otros anteriores . . . que jamás cumplieron los gobiernos; porque la substancia, el alma de tales documentos es un alma en pena que sufre su purgatorio en este mundo, pasando de ministerio a ministerio, y que ve siempre lejos . . . muy distante, el cielo en que se realizan las promesas. (p. 1)

[In parliamentary governments, each entering ministry presents its program. It's *de rigueur.* And each one of those programs resembles many other previous ones . . . that governments never executed; because the substance, the soul of such documents is a pained soul that suffers its purgatory in this world, passing from ministry to ministry, and that sees always far-off . . . very distant, the heaven in which promises are kept.]

According to Gutiérrez Nájera and Díaz Dufóo, governments and especially their documents are incapable of reaching the goals that they prescribe. By contrast, and as their alternative to the failures of bureaucratic discourse, the review's creators celebrate a new savior: "El arte es nuestro príncipe y Señor, porque el arte descifra y lee en voz alta el poema vivificante de la tierra y la harmonía del movimiento en el espacio" [Art is our prince and Lord, because art deciphers and reads aloud the life-rendering poem of the earth and the harmony of movement in space] (p. 1). Art interprets and utters the life-giving poem of the land. What better summary could there be of the cultural work that Darío sets out to accomplish in "Salutación del optimista"? Regarding the *modernistas'* rhetorical use of religious commonplaces to advocate an autonomous space for the arts, Angel Rama observes:

La religión del arte es la forma ideológica de la especialización provo-
cada por la división del trabajo, en un momento en que ha quebrado
el público real. Y el idealismo renaniano y el esteticismo, los únicos
asideros autónomos que en primera instancia descubren los poetas
como territorios propios que les permiten justificarse y redefinir su
función social. (*Rubén Darío y el modernismo,* p. 48).

[The religion of art is the ideological form of specialization provoked
by the division of labor, in a moment in which the real public has split.
And Renan's idealism and aestheticism, the only autonomous pretexts
that the poets discover in the first instance as territories of their own
that permit them to justify themselves and redefine their social function.]

In his engagement with Dürkheim's theory of religion, Jameson illustrates how such a bid for autonomy theoretically might function:

Indeed, to theorize religion as an "eternal" drive by which social divisions are suspended or overcome, to propose religious and ritual practices as a symbolic way of affirming social unity in a society which is
objectively class divided, is clearly an ideological operation and an
attempt to conjure such divisions away by an appeal to some higher
(and imaginary) principle of collective and social unity. To stress the
purely *symbolic* character of such unification, however, is to place this
theory in a perspective in which religious practices and cultural production – the nostalgia for the collective and the Utopian – are har-
nessed to ideological ends. (*The Political Unconscious,* p. 292)

The reviews' creators use a language of religious faith and conver-
sion in order to promote the unanimity of their endeavors and to
extend their influence beyond the limits of a professional "we."
These strategies are clearly visible in perhaps the most cited of the
modernista manifestos – the opening remarks of the *Revista de
América.*

In its first issue (August 19, 1894), Rubén Darío and Ricardo

Jaimes Freyre, like Gutiérrez Nájera and Díaz Dufóo, declare their allegiance to a cult of pure art and attempt to recruit "followers" from the rest of Spanish America. The first clause of the inaugural remarks, "Nuestros propósitos," states that the review proposes to be "el órgano de la generación nueva que en América profesa el culto del Arte puro, y desea y busca la perfección ideal" [the organ of the new generation that professes the cult of pure Art in America, and desires and seeks ideal perfection] (p. 1). The second proclaims their ambitious desire to become "el vínculo que haga una y fuerte la idea americana en la universal comunión artística" [the bond that unites and strengthens the American idea in universal artistic communion] (p. 1). Both statements designate a utopia in which "la idea americana" (an imagined, transnational community) merges with a universal communion of artists. It is precisely through this sublime union that the literary is supposed to gain its autonomous status and, moreover, in the same instant that the idea of America comes into being. Besides indicating their aesthetic and transnational agendas, Darío and Jaimes Freyre also take this opportunity to identify their "enemies." They vow to "combatir contra los fetichistas y contra los iconoclastas" [fight against the fetishists and against the iconoclasts] and "luchar porque prevalezca el amor a la divina Belleza, tan combatido hoy por invasoras tendencias utilitarias" [struggle so that the love of divine Beauty may prevail, so attacked today by invading utilitarian tendencies] (p. 1). The editors of the *Revista de América* advocate a quest for a pure art that in practice can be attained only through the erasure of competing discourses. The belligerent tone of this language – not far removed from the "violence and precision" formula that Marinetti used for his art of manifesto writing (see Perloff) – is compounded and discursively organized by one trope in particular: the religious pilgrimage.[8] Darío and Jaimes Freyre state their readiness to:

Levantar oficialmente la bandera de la peregrinación estética que hoy hace con visible esfuerzo, la juventud de la América latina, a los Santos lugares del Arte y a los desconocidos Orientes del ensueño;
Mantener, al propio tiempo que el pensamiento de la innovación, el respeto a las tradiciones y la gerarquía de los maestros;

Trabajar por el brillo de la lengua castellana en América, y, al par que por el tesoro de sus riquezas antiguas, por el engrandecimiento de esas mismas riquezas en vocabulario, rítmica, plasticidad y matiz. (p. 1)[9]

[Officially raise the banner of aesthetic pilgrimage that Latin American youth today makes with visible effort, to the Holy places of Art and to dream's unknown Orients;

Maintain, at the same time as the thought for innovation, respect for traditions and the hierarchy of the masters;

Work on behalf of the brilliance of the Castilian tongue in America, and, at the same time for the treasure of its ancient riches, for the aggrandizement of those same riches in vocabulary, rhythm, plasticity and nuance.]

According to this manifesto, the aesthetic pilgrimage can accomplish two goals. Although at first glance they both appear to be related in a contradictory manner, together they accurately reveal the peculiar, postcolonial circumstances of Spanish American *modernismo*. The first goal corresponds to the outward journey of Spanish America's youth in search of "la perfección ideal." It aligns itself with the general notion of aesthetic and social progress that we have seen in these manifestos and in Rodó's *Ariel*; its watchword is "innovación." The second goal, however, reiterates the importance of respecting traditions, conserving hierarchies, and refining the Castilian tongue in the Americas.

In their ideological function, the *modernistas'* symbolic pilgrimages appropriately capture the notion of a journey toward the presumed "certainty" of sanctified places of art, toward utopian spaces of pure literary language and an eventual return. In "Literary History and Literary Modernity," de Man outlines a movement in modern literature that is reminiscent of the *modernistas'* symbolic pilgrimages. "Literature," he writes,

can be represented as a movement and is, in essence, the fictional narration of this movement. After the initial moment of flight away from its own specificity, a moment of return follows that leads literature back to what it is – but we must bear in mind that terms such as "after" and "follows" do not designate actual moments in a diachrony, but are used purely as *metaphors* of duration. (p. 159)

Because they could freely appreciate (objectify and incorporate) cultural artifacts from the locally produced and "foreign" texts that they read, the *modernistas* moved away from certain hegemonic, "literary essences" and returned to those essences by trying to renew them. Here lies the radical impetus of Darío's and Jaimes Freyre's quest for an ideal art. Their pilgrimage in search of a purer artistic expression does not necessarily represent a desire to undertake such a journey but, rather, constitutes an attempt at self-definition. The symbolic nature of this journey and self-definition is aptly described by Johnson when she writes that "if u-topia (no place) and the common-place are ultimately indistinguishable . . . it can only be because the truly unreachable utopian place, the place which is par excellence unknowable, is not some faraway mysterious land, but the very place where *one is*" (p. 41).

As the central trope in the *Revista de América*'s manifesto and as a commonplace in others, the pilgrimage does not imply rupture and absolute separation from former (colonial) traditions and practices but a willingness on the part of the reviews' creators to participate in them as historical subjects. The appropriation and reworking of symbolic religious practices represents an aggressive artistic stance in the face of undesirable historical (and historio-graphical) circumstances. Octavio Paz observes that the use of reli-gious codes is part of an important *modernista* agenda. He argues that the object of the *modernistas*' passion is directly linked to their attitude toward history: "El amor a la modernidad no es culto a la moda: es voluntad de participación en una plenitud histórica hasta entonces vedada a los hispanoamericanos" [The love of modernity is not homage to fashion: it is the will to participate in a historical plenitude forbidden until then to Hispano-Americans] (*Cuadrivio*, p. 21). This critical approach assigns a conscious, participatory role to the *modernista* writing of Spanish America's history and to its "new" historians. "Recapitulando la empresa martiana," Aníbal González similarly points out, "Darío quiso hallar la manera de dominar la entropía y, sobre todo, de 'curar' la historia, rellenando sus fisuras y discontinuidades, de tal forma que ésta pudiese seguir adelante" [Recapitulating Martí's enterprise, Darío attempted to find the way to dominate entropy and, above all, to "cure" history, filling its fissures and discontinuities, in such a way that the latter could carry on] (*La crónica modernista hispanoamericana*, pp. 145–6).

This image of an aesthetics that miraculously serves to cure history appears in the first issue of *Cosmópolis*. Its creators claim: "Rubén Darío, Gutiérrez Nájera, Gómez Carrillo, Julián del Casal y tantos otros dan vida a nuestra habla castellana, y hacen correr calor y luz por las venas de nuestro idioma que se moria [sic] de anemia y parecía condenado a sucumbir como un viejo decrépito y gastado" [Rubén Darío, Gutiérrez Nájera, Gómez Carrillo, Julián del Casal, and so many others give life to our Castilian speech, and cause warmth and light to run through the veins of our language that was dying of anemia and seemed condemned to succumb like a decrepit and spent old man] (Coll et al., p. 4). The *modernistas* participate in history through writing and by positing themselves in the most strategic position from which they can affect the development of the Spanish language and its literatures. In this respect, it is not arbitrary that when the editors of the *Revista de América* picture themselves raising the banner of aesthetic pilgrimage, they open their discourse to all the resonances (and renewal) of the literature of Reconquest and Discovery.

Whereas the editors of the *Revista de América* proclaim their crusade, those of *Cosmópolis* already seem to behold their utopia. Of all the editorial groups mentioned in this study, Pedro Coll and his colleagues imagine the most extensive, transnational, cultural space. In the first issue, they claim for their pages a "beautiful" form of civilization that transcends not only prejudices but the nation as well:

En este periódico como lo indica su nombre tendrán acogida todas las escuelas literarias, de todos los países. El cosmopolitismo es una de las formas más hermosas de la civilización pues que ella reconoce que el hombre rompiendo con preocupaciones y prejuicios, remplaza la idea de Patria por la de Humanidad.

La literatura ha hecho en favor de la confraternidad humana más que todas las intrigas diplomáticas; los países más lejanos se conocen, se acercan y simpatizan por el libro y el periódico; las ideas viajan de una nación a otra sin hacer caso de los empleados de aduana, ni de los ejércitos fronterizos, las razas se estrechan, y la Paz se impone. (Coll et al., pp. 3–4)

[In this newspaper as its name indicates all literary schools from every country will be welcomed. Cosmopolitanism is one of the most beautiful forms of civilization, for it recognizes that man breaking with worries and prejudices, replaces the idea of Patria with that of Humanity.

Literature has done on behalf of human brotherhood more than all the diplomatic intrigues; the most distant countries meet, approach and take to one another through the book and newspaper; ideas travel from one nation to another without paying heed to Customs' officials, nor to frontier armies, races reach out and Peace imposes itself.]

According to Coll and his cohorts, the utopia that *Cosmópolis'* pages can provide opens up a new discursive space in which all literary schools from all countries are welcomed. Differences are conjured away. In this case, a process of recognition that prescribes that individuals liberate themselves from certain preoccupations and prejudices erases these (national) differences. That the review's creators privilege literature over diplomatic intrigues harkens once again to our previous observations on the autonomy of literary discourse; that they also imagine a literary peace imposing itself while the world's races embrace one another is a celebration of this independence.

However, despite their promotion of the universality of literature, *Cosmópolis'* founders also insist that they are rooted in a local space. As if he came to realize the unbridled nature of their momentum toward universality, one of the founders suddenly recalls the movement's point of departure: "desaparece el nombre de patria y queda humanidad: el arte universal; la santa y última expresión de la confraternidad artística. ¡Pero diablos! admito el programa siempre que vibra en él la nota criolla. ¡Regionalismo! ¡Regionalismo! . . . ¡Patria! Literatura nacional que brote fecunda del vientre virgen de la patria" [the name patria disappears and humanity remains: universal art; the holy and ultimate expression of artistic brotherhood. But by Jove! I admit the program so long as the Creole note vibrates in it. Regionalism! Regionalism! . . . Patria! National literature that emerges fecund from the patria's virgin womb] (p. 5). This distancing from and return to the point of departure has important consequences for the creators and readers of the utopian space that this manifesto promotes. It suggests the possibility of belonging to national and transnational spaces simultaneously and, moreover, without contradiction. The movement from the local to the cosmopolitan is also implied by the last appropriation of biblical symbolism, in which the patria's virgin womb gives birth to a national literature that comes to light in a state of fertility – that is, predisposed toward immediate regional and international dissemination. National literatures, from the perspective of the *Revista de América*'s creators, seem obliged to "depart from" the national community in order to define the nation from outside its borders. This ability to define from without is precisely what empowered the region's ruling classes within their respective countries. The "nota criolla," in other words, must remain a vital force if the cosmopolitan program is to succeed. This Creole cosmopolitanism defines the transnational cultural identity that linked the region's ruling classes. In the final instance, these discourses of class and regional identity are inextricably bound.

The *modernista* approach to nation-building was founded on a manipulative and specifically pedagogical ruling-class ideology. At the turn of the century, the attitude that culture could be objectified and modeled according to prescribed ideals was an important political theory among leaders and intellectuals in the Americas as well as in Europe. Naturally, the literary presses and newspapers that sought out an influential reading public did not disseminate a notion of an "idea americana" that was accessible to all. Therefore, the interpretation that economic and technological progress in Spanish America facilitated a universal expression of patriotic sentiments is at best partial. The assumption that underlies this view is that the expansion of the press in the region necessarily democratized the access to constructions of cultural identity. Although the spread of the press at the turn of the century theoretically implies that a democratization of information systems had occurred (see Julio Ramos, p. 101), it cannot account for the discriminating appeal that the literary reviews made to the ruling classes in Spanish American societies. By assuming that they should have defined a Hispanic identity corresponding to a contemporary appreciation for economic liberalism, the *modernistas* and their cultural agendas are doomed a priori to an aesthetics that inherently resists dissemination. From this perspective, their movement cannot stand on its own – that is, be judged according to its own criteria. Moreover, by theorizing *modernismo* as a manifestation of Spanish America's ability to catch up with the rest of the developed world, some of the critics I have mentioned posit and elaborate the *modernistas'* subjectivity in direct proportion to a period of economic prosperity and early industrialization. In addition to their quantification of culture, Anderson's views on nationalism in particular justify the insinuation that the nation-building experience can be evaluated according to the absolute values of economic success and failure. The currency of these critical claims subjugates the Spanish American *modernista* text to a discourse always in excess or evacuated of cultural meaning.

6

The "excesses" of Spanish American *modernismo*

In this study, I have looked at some of the criticism that has been written about Spanish American *modernismo* and focused my attention on one of the major currents within this field in order to interrogate its insistence that the movement's members eluded the communities in which they lived. My attempts to contextualize this current both historically and critically were motivated by what I saw as a need to develop an interpretive approach to the movement's aesthetics that would not erase the politics of culture that the *modernistas* conceived and implemented in and through their writings. I have conceptualized "detachment," therefore, not as an intentional flight from power but as a social imaginary that appears to be constructed and exercised from outside and above the greater part of Spanish American societies. However, to continue to assert today that the *modernistas* had little or no interest in defining their surroundings can reveal, in my opinion, a critical discomfort that closely resembles Doris Sommer's identification of an anxiety of influence on the part of the Boom writers toward the authors of Spanish America's foundational novels.[1] Is it also possible to speak of an anxiety of influence to qualify the relationship between the *modernistas* – the first institutionally supported commentators on Western cultures in the region – and today's literary and cultural critics of Spanish American letters? It had been fruitful to pose this question in the form of an academic project: In light of the general consensus that the movement represented the first transnational expression of cultural identity in the region, why was there such an aversion among some of the movement's critics to considering the *modernistas* the first collective and autochthonous producers of this expression? I chose to answer this question by indicating how the

modernistas produced literature about their culture(s) and by illustrating some of the ways in which they performed and promoted
these discourses in the "public spaces" of turn-of-the-century
Spanish America and Spain. Nevertheless, there are connections
(yet to be adequately investigated) between the *modernistas* and
today's critics precisely because we share with them a concern for
the politics of discursively constructing Spanish Americanness.
Although one of my goals in this study was to trace an intellectual
heritage from Darío, Martí, Gutiérrez Nájera, Rodó, and others, my
implicit aim has also been to suggest that by distancing ourselves
from the *modernistas'* ideology of culture, we run two related risks.
First, by not examining their practices as socially significant, we end
up implying that this ideology was transparent and, for that reason,
expedient. Second, by failing to posit their privileged sites of enunciation as a field of political practice, we can be accused in turn of
camouflaging our status as contemporary definers and critics of
culture. These risks are connected because, as it should be
apparent by now, our critical inquiries and bibliographies validate
their works and canonization in a variety of ways.

Far from condoning the *modernistas'* attitude toward their cultures, as a literary critic I still had to grapple with the following
issue. If it can be generally agreed that the movement's members
invoked through their art the splendors of the Spanish Conquest,
European Renaissance and Romanticism, the Enlightenment, the
allure of nineteenth-century Paris, and so on, how does one contextualize the production of that social imaginary in Spanish
America? As I indicated at the beginning of this study, one way had
been to sever the *modernistas* ideologically from their societies. This
circumvention of the problem marked a false frontier of critical
analysis in the field. To the extent that this approach is still preva-
lent, the type of question that it avoids is, Who produced this social
imaginary and for whom? In a more detailed analysis, it would be
worthwhile to inquire, How did the principal figures practice this
aesthetics? What state, social, and commercial organizations supported them? Who did they compete against and why? With
respect to their addressees, one could ask, Who appreciated – in
other words, stood to gain, encouraged, criticized, or debunked –

the *modernistas'* art? And, What were their motives in that evaluation? These questions that directly deal with the creation of an aesthetic discourse in a particular time and place are put aside when
avoidance remains the movement's overriding characteristic.
From the perspective of the escapist detachment hypothesis, for
example, the *modernistas* were considered aloof and deviant.
According to some critics, these artists possessed addictive personalities, suffered depressions, social and economic embarrassments,
bouts of jealousy and rage – all of which supposedly accentuated
their already acute sensibilities. This attention to the pathological
conduct of artists in the public sphere encourages the reduction of
real social conflicts to biographical peculiarities; it limits the place
of the arts in a society to unpredictable combinations of social
malaise, talent, and erratic behavior. As a critical language, it
cannot even begin to address definitions of culture. How interesting it would be to use these adjectives and human circumstances
to describe instead the emergence and social specificity of an aesthetic discourse and, moreover, to contextualize the incipient production of this discourse in a period of transnational definitions of
Spanish American culture!

To conclude this study, I would like to summarize the close readings that I have offered by bringing them to bear on a discussion
of a particular *modernista* aesthetic practice and its relevance to
Spanish American cultural autonomy. This practice can be sum-
marized in the observation by *modernistas*, their critics, and other
members of the reading public that the movement's followers
emphasized (for some, overemphasized) an embellished language
and a concurrent "importation" of European cultural signs. That a
literary language should be thus fashioned caused a debate in
which advocates argued that this attention to form constituted a
renewal, a revolution of sorts in Spanish-language poetry, and
opponents maintained that the *modernistas* created empty signs, as
Juan Valera said of Darío's *Azul.* Unless otherwise qualified, I refer
to the movement's aesthetic practice as an expertise in the selection, use, and specialized treatment of a wide range of cultural
signs and, above all, to a conscious cultivation of that expertise by
exquisite design. When I allude to "Spanish American cultural

autonomy," I am describing the *modernistas'* discursive construction of a specific geocultural community around the turn of the century. This community is not imagined passively, as in Anderson's *Imagined Communities*, but is purposefully constructed through a symbolic, utopian discourse. The connections between this discourse and the community that subscribes to it result from the interpellation of an elite group of national and transnational readers and an inculcation in these readers of a belief in the imminence of and need for – in the words of the *Revista de América*'s manifesto – "la idea americana." This final chapter concentrates on the contexts of a literary language used to signify Spanish American culture. My concluding hypothesis is that those qualities that have been characterized in *modernista* aesthetics as empty signs, art for art's sake, the esoteric, the ephemeral, *volupté*, the preoccupation with fashion, auras, and fleeting impressions, were in fact the ways in which the *modernistas* registered their experience of the modern. Although they wrote from the "peripheries" of Western civilization, their records of this experience nonetheless corroborate Marx's famous observation on the consequences of the rise of the bourgeoisie that "all that is solid melts into air, all that is holy is profaned" (p. 476). I regard these inscriptions, therefore, as a mostly urban and transnational practice and argue that this class-grounding experience of the modern informed the movement's expression of a postcolonial cultural identity. In making these claims, I bear in mind de Man's view that at various moments in history, "the topic 'modernity' might be used just as an attempt at self-definition, as a way of diagnosing one's own present" ("Literary History and Literary Modernity," p. 143), and I employ it to elucidate the *modernistas'* idealized definitions of Spanish America at the turn of the century.

The emergence of a literary language

I began this study by stating my reasons for employing certain contemporary approaches to the study of Spanish American *modernismo*. The first and foremost reason pleaded the obvious – that it is impossible to extricate oneself from a particular moment to "reconstruct" another historical period. Perhaps the most evident use of such an approach was my poststructuralist reading of "Salutación del optimista." Homi Bhabha's essay, "DissemiNation: Time, Narrative, and the Margins of the Modern Nation," was useful for this reading because it allowed me to highlight a suspension of cultural meaning between the pan-Hispanic people's rhetorical strategies of self-generation and "their" self-enunciation through the poem's language. "Cultural difference," Bhabha argues, "is to be found where the 'loss' of meaning enters, as a cutting edge, into the representation of the fullness of the demands of a culture" (p. 313). My analysis of this cutting edge and suspension of meaning took as its point of departure the premise that today we read "Salutación del optimista" as a text. Yet, because treating the poem as if it were a text alone is a shortcoming, it was essential to illustrate that the poem's cultural meaning also resided in its historical performance before a specific audience. In this two-pronged approach, the tension between my poststructuralist reading of the poem and the poet's recitation emerged: Darío had never intended to "suspend cultural meaning," but he could within the specificity of his performance earnestly try to convince listeners of the splendor of the pan-Hispanic community that he envisaged and promoted.

So what is to be gained in a poststructuralist approach to this *modernista* cultural text? The most important advantage is that if we assume that a community's fullest self-expression can never be more absolute than an interrupted address, then it is possible to consider "Salutación del optimista" a valid attempt in its own right to define a cultural identity precisely because this accomplishment lies in the *strategic approximations and incommensurabilities* of that identity. (By contrast, the evasive detachment hypothesis presumes the absolute commensurability of national borders, cultural identity, and literary expression.) Efforts in the poem to create a unique *raza* by suturing into an organic whole references to the legendary pasts of imperial Rome and Spain and the future promise of Spanish America at the turn of the century are examples of such strategies. They describe what Nietzsche calls the "*plastic power* of a man, a people, a culture" – that is, "the capacity to develop out of oneself in one's own way, to transform and incorporate into oneself what is past and foreign, to heal wounds, to replace what has been lost, to recreate broken moulds" (p. 62). The symbolic attempts to transcend the geography and history of the Atlantic are informed by a utopian design and its inherent shortcomings; they manifest themselves in the very closures that they are meant to and cannot enforce. In this respect, the agenda to forge a pan-Hispanic community in "Salutación del optimista" illustrates what Ernesto Laclau calls the ideological – that is, "those discursive forms through which a society tries to institute itself as such on the basis of closure, of the fixation of meaning, *of the non-recognition of the infinite play of differences*" (*New Reflections on the Revolution of Our Time*, p. 92; emphasis added). The assertion that a society tries to found itself by attempting to fix meaning throws an interesting light on the *modernistas'* definitions of Spanish American and pan-Hispanic cultures. Since they operated within an intellectual tradition that valorized cultural identities and their literary expressions according to their "purity" (or lack thereof), the *modernistas* were eager to fix meanings not only because they were aware of participating in that tradition and thus empowering themselves from the "periphery" but also because they had to negotiate the cultural value of these meanings in the penumbra of a colonial past. Paz rightly associates the *modernistas'* aesthetic practice with a bid for cultural autonomy when he states (and it is worth repeating) that "el amor a la modernidad no es culto a la moda: es voluntad de participación en una plenitud histórica hasta entonces vedada a los hispanoamericanos" [the love of modernity is not homage to fashion: it is the will to participate in a historical plenitude forbidden until then to Hispano-Americans] (*Cuadrivio*, p. 21). In other words, the "peripheral" location of the Spanish American *modernistas* and their transnational community on the fringes of European intellectual traditions and civilization made these artists and intellectuals some of the first non-European cultural workers to construct and fix meanings locally by objectifying, assimilating, and thereby deterritorializing the "center's" cultural signs.

As I have shown, this deterritorialization of European artifacts and traditions met with immediate and often vehement opposition. Eagleton points out that a commercially viable, free, and open market ensures the assimilability of literary texts, thereby weakening the capability of any culture to produce an idiosyncratic expression of its uniqueness. Among the first in a long tradition, critics and contemporaries of the movement like Juan Valera and José Enrique Rodó elaborated the stereotype that because these artists had "imported" these artifacts and traditions in order to supplement and lend credibility to their community's self-expression, the *modernistas* either vacated or exceeded their own cultural locations and merely indulged in the "excesses" of art for art's sake. The competition between Darío and Rodó to be the spokesman for Spanish American cultural independence illustrates this point. Although both sought to formulate a language that would correspond to this quest for autonomy, Rodó rejected the *modernistas'* art by claiming that they employed a particular superficiality and frivolity and that Darío, through this practice, had exhibited an involuntary anti-Americanism. These critics associated the language that the community must use to refer to itself with the appropriateness of signifiers in the text. In short, with respect to Spanish American *modernismo*, the relation that the signifier maintained with the signified became an issue of cultural politics in which the language of identity and difference that was used to stabilize and naturalize the cultural sign became a battleground among poets, writers, and their critics. Strategies to privilege forms of cultural meaning not only played out class conflicts and allegiances as they were being experienced and inscribed by particular groups but were also informed and deeply affected by the memory and aftermath of a recent colonial past. From the perspective of this conflictive semiotics of cultural meaning, it is easier to comprehend how the *modernistas'* art could be subversive and why, for example, Pedro Salinas chose to safeguard his literary and cultural values by disparagingly calling the movement a poetic practice in which the *modernistas* have access to an extraordinary variety of referents but fail to conserve a Hispanic essence or *raza*.

The anxiety that the deterritorialization of European cultural artifacts caused is inadvertently well documented among those observers who insisted in the *modernistas'* aloofness. This insistence took the form of ethical and aesthetic determinations that these artists and intellectuals ultimately had no right to "import" cultural objects that belonged to other countries for Spanish American consumption; what it in fact camouflaged was the disturbing realization that the *modernistas* had indeed been successful at creating a particular social imaginary and, furthermore, that in doing so their aesthetic practices had exposed precisely how national cultures were and could be constructed through language. By illustrating the *constructedness* and fragmentary nature of identities, Darío and others threatened to destabilize privileged and/or imposed signs of cultural meaning; they shifted attention away from the essence of cultures – as Salinas, Díaz Plaja, and other critics maintained – to their material representations. This focus on imaging and the creation of identity is evident, for instance, in Darío's poetic language. In her analysis of his early poetic voices, Molloy comments on Darío's coupling of subjectivity and appearance in a manner that aptly addresses the emergence of Spanish American *modernismo* as a discourse of cultural identity:

Darío postula una persona más atenta a la apariencia que a su esencia, más preocupada por la manera en que ha de expresarse que por lo que la constituye. De estos primeros ejemplos podría decirse que más que verdaderas personas son simulacros de personas, simples vehículos de una voz poética que aún no se encuentra: verdaderos *shifters* en un enunciado fluctuante. ("Conciencia del público y conciencia del yo en el primer Darío," p. 445)

[Darío postulates a personage more attentive to appearance than to essence, more concerned by the manner in which it must be expressed than by what constitutes it. Of those first examples it could be said that more than true personages they are simulacra of personages, mere vehicles of a poetic voice that is yet to be found: true *shifters* in a fluctuating enunciation.]

Molloy's notion that a poetic voice – that is to say, the creation of a poetic subject – is composed of a series of shifters, also resonates in Laclau's and Mouffe's argument that "society and social agents lack any essence, and their regularities merely consist of the relative and precarious form of fixation which accompany the establishment of a certain order" (p. 98).

This precariousness of subject positions is well illustrated in "El rey burgués" ["The Bourgeois King"], Darío's most famous short story. The short story itself may be read not only as the plight of a troubled poet but as the shifting coordinates of an aesthetic and intellectual practice peculiar to its time and place. In the text, the disenfranchised though idealistic poet/protagonist enters the exquisite court of the monarch and complains that the integrity of his literature has been placed under siege by those below and above his station. No longer the composer of "grandes himnos," the poet has come down in the world to suffer the humiliation of wage labor. The accord that the Bourgeois King strikes with the protagonist is unequivocal: "Pieza de música por pedazo de pan" [A piece of music for a piece of bread] (p. 20). And it is against this background of a displaced social status and the professionalization of his art that the poet searches for a permanent subjectivity and closure. His only speech, which can be read as an attempt to define a stable discursive ground, is characterized by a mesmerizing multiplicity of once inhabited subject positions; at the same time, it tells the tale of a poetic language in search of a privileged social meaning:

yo canto el verbo del porvenir. He tendido mis alas al huracán, he nacido en el tiempo de la aurora; busco la raza escogida. . . . He abandonado la inspiración de la ciudad malsana. . . . He roto el arpa adulona de las cuerdas débiles . . . he arrojado el manto que me hacía parecer histrión o mujer, y he vestido de modo salvaje y espléndido. . . . He ido a la selva, donde he quedado vigoroso y ahíto de leche fecunda y licor de nueva vida. . . .

He acariciado a la gran Naturaleza, y he buscado el calor ideal, el verso que está en el astro, en el fondo del cielo, y el que está en la perla, en lo profundo del océano. ("El rey burgués," p. 19)

[I sing the word of the future. I have spread my wings before the hurricane, I have come to life in dawn's season; I search for the chosen race. . . . I have abandoned the unclean city's inspiration. . . . I have smashed the adulating feeble-stringed harp . . . I have thrown off the cloak that made me appear a histrion or woman, and I have dressed in a savage and splendid way. . . . I have gone to the jungle, where I have been made vigorous and satiated by enriching milk and the liqueur of new life. . . .

I have caressed great Nature, and I have sought ideal warmth, the verse that is in the star, at the back of the sky, and the one that is in the pearl, in the depths of the ocean.]

This quest for a permanent subjectivity raises a variety of issues, including the prophetic capabilities of the poet (and poetry), the search for a chosen community or *raza*, the ambiguous shift from cities to nature as the source of poetic inspiration, the rejection of a "weak" lyricism, and the concurrent gendering of that rejection. More than a dramatic display of loss and powerlessness, the repeated self-enunciations mark a perennially shifting, discursive landscape and a conscious effort to establish the boundaries of class as well as cultural meaning.

In the final analysis, that Spanish American *modernistas* seemed capable of producing only imprecise or inferior copies of European cultural artifacts and signs should not dissuade us from elucidating the manner in which they introduced these objects and meanings into their societies. In today's critical climate, it is possible to associate those approximations and incommensurabilities with the poststructuralist emphasis on the ultimate impossibility of fixed meaning. This conflation permits me to reassess the *modernistas'* "excesses," their so-called production of empty signs, and posit a subjectivity that emerges to contest a colonial past.

The postcoloniality of Spanish American modernismo

If the deterritorialization of cultural signs illustrates the constructedness of national and transnational cultures, then this *modernista* practice must also be evaluated as a proper response to the literary traditions of the region's colonizers. I noted in his recitation of "Salutación del optimista" and in their anticipation of a potential reading public that Darío and the creators of the *modernista* literary reviews were aware that the moment had arrived to participate in a historical fullness previously forbidden to Spanish Americans. Do the writings inspired by this state of awareness constitute a post-colonial literature? In determining the postcoloniality of these texts (that is, the degree to which they resist, subvert, and/or abrogate the colonizer's codes) according to the acquisition of political independence by the countries in which they were produced, then, with the exception of literature from Cuba and Puerto Rico, what Spanish Americans wrote after Spain had lost most of its colonies in the first quarter of the nineteenth century must be regarded as postcolonial. Yet political independence is an inadequate yardstick with which to measure the postcoloniality of a literature. For example, one need only examine the inaugural remarks and pages of *La Habana Elegante* and *La Habana Literaria* to notice the extent to which the cultural politics of these Cuban publications coincides with that of reviews in other parts of Spanish America before and after its independence in 1898. The forging of a culture or "patrimonio común" – as the general director of Seville's Expo '92, Manuel Olivencia, implied – is a project that goes beyond the "fixed meanings" of statecraft and geopolitical borders. In Gutiérrez Nájera's denunciation of parliamentary procedure in the *Revista Azul's* opening remarks and in the *Cosmópolis'* simultaneous celebration of literature and belittling of diplomatic intrigue, it was not uncommon to find among *modernista* artists and intellectuals the creed that literary discourse was better suited to defining Spanish American culture than the language of state politics.

In this study, I have illustrated how cultural meanings were constructed and promoted across national borders and in dialogue with the literary production of Europe and to a lesser extent with that of the United States. However, any discussion of Spanish American *modernismo*'s status as a postcolonial, literary movement must account for a difficult theoretical issue: If resistance to colonizers forms one of the principal characteristics of a postcolonial subjectivity, what can be said about the *modernistas'* stated appreciation for Europe's metropolitan cultures and art? How can one rationalize the *Revista de América's* seemingly paradoxical vow to innovate, to revolutionize on the one hand and respect "las tradiciones y la gerarquía de los maestros" [the traditions and hierarchy of the masters] on the other? What was its motive in working toward "el brillo de la lengua castellana en América" [the brilliance of the Castilian tongue in America]? Postcolonial literary theory today is intimately tied to recent experiences of political and cultural decolonization in which forms of resistance to the colonizer's tongue (and its political, socioeconomic, and cultural infrastructures) appear to be the norm. These forms of resistance or contestation also have a theoretical counterpart that regards the use of "European theory" to explicate non-European contexts as an imposition or even a kind of neocolonialism. In *The Empire Writes Back*, Ashcroft, Griffiths, and Tiffin argue that "the idea of 'post-colonial literary theory' emerges from the inability of European theory to deal adequately with the complexities and varied cultural provenance of post-colonial writing" (p. 11). (The notion that the *modernistas* did not wield power in their societies is to a certain extent an example of that inadequacy. To support this claim, it would be necessary to show how "European theory" can also be deterritorialized, appropriated, and indigenized by theorists in non-European countries.) What cannot be denied is that the *modernistas* attempted from above to revolutionize Spanish-language literature through their active participation in a cosmopolitan trade in cultural referents. In their intertextual construction of a Spanish American social imaginary, the movement's writers and poets sought to establish cultural parity with Europe and superiority over Anglo-Saxon America. Their concern, as Darío eloquently espoused in "Salutación del optimista," was not to break with European Culture but to supplement it by representing Spanish America as the time and place of Europe's cultural posterity. This cultural *rapprochement* with the continent that colonized the Americas can be considered an attempt to join a global order (and hegemony) as a full and equal participant, and from this perspective, it is a bold response to a colonial past.[2] When Ashcroft, Griffiths, and Tiffin conclude that "the process of literary decolonization has involved a radical dismantling of the European codes and a post-colonial subversion and appropriation of the dominant European discourses" (p. 195), their words also ring true for the *modernistas*' aesthetic practice. Nevertheless, rather than lay down a radical rule in a new and dynamic field that the complete abrogation of all things imperial and imposed is the foremost prerequisite for a postcolonial literature, I will postulate how Spanish American *modernismo* may fall under this rubric. In order to do so, I will summarize the connotations of the term *raza* as it is conceptualized in some of the texts that I examined in this study.

As I briefly mentioned in the Introduction, the term *raza*, or race, in nineteenth-century Spanish America did not valorize ethnic difference as a site of agency. Judging by Darío's use of the words "mulatez intelectual" (see Chapter 2) to refer to a supposed lack of preparation among his fellow Spanish American artists, representations of miscegenation could not accomplish the symbolic and cultural work that the *modernistas* envisioned. For them, the word "raza" signaled the ability of a transnational people to come into being and fulfill its manifest destiny. Its significance presupposed the integrity of cultural meaning, the ability to achieve, for example, the kind of completeness and autonomy toward which the poetic voice in "Salutación del optimista" strove as it eliminated dissent and by the end of the poem celebrated an epiphany of pan-Hispanic unity. *Raza*, therefore, represents the concretization of a pure and unchallengeable meaning and identity. By contrast, dissent and difference connoted untimeliness, distortion, and hybridity – the quality of being "ni fructuoso ni oportuno" [neither fruitful nor opportune] as Darío said of the call for an artistic manifesto in "Palabras liminares," or in need of a pedagogy that would sculpt and embellish "la arcilla humana" [human clay], as Próspero maintained in Rodó's *Ariel*. Basically, the *modernistas'* use of the word *raza* resembles Renan's definition of the nation as "a soul, a spiritual principle," and "a large-scale solidarity" ("What is a Nation?" p. 19). The French intellectual further explains his understanding of the nation in a lecture that he delivered at the Sorbonne in 1882:

A large aggregate of men, healthy in mind and warm of heart, creates the kind of moral conscience which we call a nation. So long as this moral consciousness gives proof of its strength by the sacrifices which demand the abdication of the individual to the advantage of the community, it is legitimate and has the right to exist. (p. 20)

This call for unanimity of purpose in spite of differences is the principle that underlies the *modernistas'* use of the term *raza*. It was on the basis of that principle that Darío in "Palabras liminares" could privilege without reservation his "manos de marqués" [marquis' hands] – that is, the talent and means through which he gave expression to a manipulative ideology of culture – over his part African and indigenous ancestry. In the final analysis, political consensus about the creation and future of a pan-Hispanic culture, not ethnic specificity, was what determined the contexts of the term.

Rodó's *Ariel* argued for a conception of a Spanish American *raza* that was very celebrated in its time. The essay's intellectual strength lies in its author's ability to promote a cultural identity that would retain its autonomy vis-à-vis the past that it shared with its former European colonizers and the future over which Spanish America was increasingly finding itself in competition with the United States. In order to steer this treacherous course, Rodó makes two crucial rhetorical moves. First, he praises "la obra de la Revolución" [the Revolution's work] because it legitimized Spanish America's political independence from Spain and Europe. However, since such a revolutionary spirit had also spawned the United States, his second move is to distinguish Spanish America from the United States. He does so by advocating a cultural *rapprochement* between Spanish-speaking America and Europe on the basis of transnational class alliances. Assuming the tone of Renan's classicist adaptation of Shakespeare's *The Tempest*, Rodó resorts to a language of contemplative high art and Classical and Christian epistemologies in order to vilify the United States as the distorted, savage, and materialistic Caliban in Shakespeare's play. Once Rodó opens this discursive space, the new Spanish American *raza* emerges: a Calibán that is different from Shakespeare's and Renan's, not hopeless – because it liberated itself from an imperial yoke – but still deformed human clay (p. 147) ready to be sculpted to perfection under the guidance or, rather, the pedagogy of Próspero's cultural art studio. Since, as Próspero indicates, there exists an "estética de la estructura social" [aesthetics of the social structure] (p. 49), this new *raza* must be properly fashioned in order to take its rightful place in that hierarchy.

By emphasizing that the *modernistas* attempted to invoke a pure and autonomous cultural meaning, I do not wish to deny that this version of a pan-Hispanic *raza* contained certain racist practices. However, revealing and denouncing these practices without describing what made them possible or even desirable from the perspective of their advocates can be only a partial critique of the assumptions that underlie the movement's cultural ideology. For what attempt to posit a unique cultural identity is not in the final instance characterized to some degree by an idealization of itself as the chosen race and/or by a vilification of another? In *Race, Nation, Class*, Balibar and Wallerstein point out and interrogate the contemporary view that "as far as the relation between *nationalism and racism* is concerned at present, the core of meaning contrasts a 'normal' ideology and politics (nationalism) with an 'excessive' ideology and behaviour (racism), either to oppose the two or to offer the one as the truth of the other" (p. 46). What they suggest as a more useful understanding of this relation – an understanding that I call upon to elucidate the *modernistas'* implicit conceptualization of a Spanish American *raza* – is "that racism is not an 'expression' of nationalism, but a *supplement of nationalism* or more precisely *a supplement internal to nationalism*, always in excess of it, but always indispensable to its constitution and yet always still insufficient to achieve its project" (p. 54). Although the effect might arguably be the same, the kind of "racism" that the *modernistas* practiced, therefore, was not restricted to color differentiations that presupposed an interest in ethnography but was played out in an "excess of 'purism'" (p. 59) in which class affiliation and political consensus determined membership.

It is no surprise then that the bulk of the *modernistas'* work involved explicit and implicit efforts to create a genealogy in which belonging to a burgeoning transnational class (and not to an empire that compromised their political independence) became the means through which Spanish America sought and simultaneously offered Europe cultural posterity. Genealogy, Balibar and Wallerstein argue, "is anything but a category of 'pure' nature: it is a symbolic category articulated to relative juridical notions and, first and foremost, to the legitimacy of filiation" (p. 56). This observation is corroborated by the poetic voice's supersession of the Atlantic through organic metaphors in "Salutación del optimista," the transnational assessment of common cultural values that the *modernista* reviews practiced, and the creation of a pan-Hispanic *raza* in *Ariel.* By supplementing "universal history" with the promise of Spanish America's bright future, the *modernistas* challenged Europe to extend its cultural borders; by presenting their readers with postcolonial, hyper-real versions of European culture and traditions – Darío's insistence, for example, on innovating and yet respecting the tradition of the masters, on appearing more Spanish than the Spanish – these artists and intellectuals were the first to create a collectively derived discursive space of Spanish American cultural identity.

Literal readings of some of the *modernistas'* texts and aesthetic tracts have led to a dismissive attitude toward the social relevance of their work. These texts have consequently been considered unreadable literature in today's modern world. Although such a conclusion may be a question of personal taste, its inscription by literary critics whose responsibilities include deciphering the works of a literary movement that was so clearly associated with the Spanish American "patrimonio común" at the beginning of this century requires further investigation. So long as the works of past and present literary movements can be used (and reused) to politicize the reading public, it behooves the critic to go beyond the question of the author's "real intent." When we read that Darío depicts himself as a cloistered monk who busies himself with the drawing of letters in a missal, we can either scoff at such examples of his wild imagination or attempt to reconstruct them in a manner that would reveal not only the intentionality but also the unconscious play of ideological motives and agendas within his language. It is by taking the *modernista* contributions to the idea and figure of Spanish America seriously – and not by erasing their relevance to those constructions – that it becomes possible to rationalize and historicize some of today's politicized perspectives on the region's culture.

Appendix

Salutación del optimista

1 Ínclitas razas ubérrimas, sangre de Hispania fecunda,
   espíritus fraternos, luminosas almas, ¡salve!
   Porque llega el momento en que habrán de cantar nuevos himnos
   lenguas de gloria. Un vasto rumor llena los ámbitos; mágicas
5 ondas de vida van renaciendo de pronto;
   retrocede el olvido, retrocede engañada la muerte;
   se anuncia un nuevo reino, feliz sibila sueña
   y en la caja pandórica de que tantas desgracias surgieron
   encontramos de súbito, talismánica, pura, riente,
10 cual pudiera decirla en sus versos Virgilio divino,
   la divina reina de luz, ¡la celeste Esperanza!

   Pálidas indolencias, desconfianzas fatales que a tumba
   o a perpetuo prisidio condenasteis al noble entusiasmo,
   ya veréis al salir del sol en un triunfo de liras,
15 mientras dos continentes, abonados de huesos gloriosos,
   del Hércules antiguo la gran sombra soberbia evocando,
   digan al orbe: la alta virtud resucita
   que a la hispana progenie hizo dueña de siglos.

   Abominad la boca que predice desgracias eternas,
20 abominad los ojos que ven sólo zodiacos funestos,
   abominad las manos que apedrean las ruinas ilustres,
   o que la tea empuña o la daga suicida.
   Siéntense sordos ímpetus de las entrañas del mundo,
   la inminencia de algo fatal hoy conmueve a la tierra;

25   fuertes colosos caen, se desbandan bicéfalas águilas,
     y algo se inicia como vasto social cataclismo
     sobre la faz del orbe. ¿Quién dirá que las savias dormidas
     no despierten entonces en el tronco del roble gigante
     bajo el cual se exprimió la ubre de la loba romana?
30   ¿Quién será el pusilánime que al vigor español niegue
        músculos
     y que al alma español juzgase áptera y ciega y tullida?
     No es Babilonia ni Nínive enterrada en olvido y en polvo
     ni entre momias y piedras reina que habita el sepulcro,
     la nación generosa, coronada de orgullo inmarchito,
35   que hacia el lado del alba fija las miradas ansiosas,
     ni la que tras los mares en que yace sepulta la Atlántida,
     tiene su coro de vástagos, altos, robustos y fuertes.

     Unanse, brillen, secúndense, tantos vigores dispersos;
     formen todos un solo haz de energía ecuménica.
40   Sangre de Hispania fecunda, sólidas, ínclitas razas,
     muestren los dones pretéritos que fueron antaño su triunfo.
     Vuelva el antiguo entusiasmo, vuelva el espíritu ardiente
     que regará lenguas de fuego en esa epifanía.
     Juntas las testas ancianas ceñidas de líricos lauros
45   y las cabezas jóvenes que la alta Minerva decora,
     así los manes heroicos de los primitivos abuelos,
     de los egregios padres que abrieron el surco prístino,
     sientan los soplos agrarios de primaverales retornos
     y el rumor de espigas que inició la labor triptolémica.

50   Un continente y otro renovando las viejas prosapias,
     en espíritu unidos, en espíritu y ansias y lengua,
     ven llegar el momento en que habrán de cantar nuevos
        himnos,
     La latina estirpe verá la gran alba futura,
     en un trueno de música gloriosa millones de labios
55   saludarán la espléndida luz que vendrá del Oriente,
     Oriente augusto en donde todo lo cambia y renueva
     la eternidad de Dios, la actividad infinita.
     Y así sea Esperanza la visión permanente en nosotros,
     ¡Inclitas razas ubérrimas, sangre de Hispania fecunda!

Notes

Chapter 1

1. Although *modernismo* is a literary manifestation of modernity, it would be inaccurate to identify it uncritically with European Modernism. For useful explanations of the term in Hispanic letters, consult D. Fernández-Morera, "The Term 'Modernism' in Literary History," in *Proceedings of the Tenth Congress of the International Comparative Literature Association,* ed. Claudio Guillén, Vol. 2, *Comparative Poetics* (New York: Garland, 1985), and Ivan A. Schulman, "Reflexiones en torno a la definición del modernismo," in *Estudios críticos sobre el modernismo,* ed. Homero Castillo (Madrid: Editorial Gredos, 1968). More recently, a series of articles in Richard A. Cardwell and Bernard McGuirk, eds., *¿Qué es el modernismo?: Nueva encuesta, nuevas lecturas* (Boulder, Colo.: Society of Spanish and Spanish-American Studies, 1993), has sought to redefine and/or delve further into this terminology. For an analysis of the use of the terms "modernism" and *"modernismo"* in Peninsular approaches to the movement, consult in that collection John Butt, "Modernismo y *Modernism.*," pp. 39–58, and Germán Gullón, "Lo moderno en el modernismo," pp. 87–102. With respect to Spanish American *modernismo,* see Adam Sharman's fine analysis of the competing discourses that inform the movement and its ideologies in "Modernismo, positivismo y (des)herencia en el discurso de la historia literaria," pp. 319–38. Throughout this book, I employ the word *modernismo* to specify the movement and *modernistas* to refer to its members.

2. This revolution transformed neither entire countries nor the region. As is the case elsewhere, the growth of the bourgeoisie in Latin America did not represent the passage to a new "stage" in history. This expanding class entered into conflict with other simultaneous modes of economic and cultural production. This uneven modernity is the subject of Néstor García Canclini's discussion in "Contradicciones latinoamericanas: ¿Modernismo sin modernización?" in Cardwell's and McGuirk's collection of critical essays, pp. 371–8.

3. The term *raza* is not easily translated. As a referent for either pan-Hispanism – which would include Spain – or Spanish Americanism, it has more in common with nineteenth-century notions of homogeneous utopian collectivities, such as the one promoted in North America as Manifest Destiny, than with race and ethnicity in postcolonial discourses or with its current usage in Chicano literature and criticism. In Chapter 6 I provide a more comprehensive discussion of the *modernistas'* use of the term.

4. They are: Juan Ramón Jiménez, "El modernismo poético en España y en Hispanoamérica"; Luis Monguió, "La modalidad peruana del modernismo"; and, concerning the Argentine contributions to *modernismo*, Rafael Alberto Arrieta, "El modernismo 1893–1900." The same critical practice of associating *modernista* esthetics with geographical entities is also evident in the 1985 Congreso Internacional sobre el Modernismo Español e Hispanoamericano, Córdoba, Spain. Paralleling the contemporary discursive fragmentation of national identities, some of the sessions in this conference covered the Catalonian and Andalusian manifestations of the movement.

5. Examples that correspond to this line of investigation are Ricardo Gullón's compilation of primary sources, *El modernismo visto por los modernistas* (1980); Jorge B. Rivera's similar collection, *El escritor y la industria cultural* (1980); Aníbal González, *La crónica modernista hispanoamericana* (1983); Julio Ramos, *Desencuentros de la modernidad en América Latina* (1989); and Susana Rotker, *La invención de la crónica* (1992).

6. The modernistas frequently employed the word "esperanza" to refer to such optimism. I am not criticizing this optimism per se nor its benevolent variants but the rhetorical use of this stance to ignore or blur contradictions and promote the idea that new beginnings – that is, the end of a particular history of social antagonisms – were and are possible.

7. Salinas and others rejected this practice because it devalued privileged cultural signs. This fact leads me to suggest that the *modernistas* were perhaps some of the first non-European "postcolonial" critics because their evaluation of national literatures could not be divorced from a cosmopolitan awareness that they spoke from the "periphery."

8. In "Disjuncture and Difference in the Global Cultural Economy," Appadurai uses the phrase "the imagination as a social practice" to describe the current situation in which "the imagination has become an organized field of social practices, a form of work (both in the sense of labor and of culturally organized practice) and a form of negotiation between sites of agency ('individuals') and globally defined fields of possibility" (p. 5). I recruit this idea of the imagina-

tion as "a form of work" to interrogate the *modernistas*' cultural politics.

9. In "Criticism and Literature within the Context of a Dependent Culture," a paper presented at the Conference on Ideology and Latin American Literature, April 29, 1975, at New York University.

10. When he associates the rise of nationalism with the geographic extension of print technology, Anderson compares Spanish American regionalism unfavorably with the successful national experience of the United States' original thirteen colonies.

Chapter 2

1. In *El modernismo visto por los modernistas*, five of the six documents that Ricardo Gullón inserts into the section he subtitles "Manifiestos modernistas" are pretextual. They are Martí's prologue to the poem, "Al Niágara"; Darío's prologue to *El canto errante*, "Dilucidaciones"; and three documents that appear in the first issues of the three literary reviews *Revista de América* (1894), *Revista Nueva* (1899), and *Helios* (1903) (p. 505). Darío's prologues are often cited as instrumental texts for outlining a Spanish American *modernista* agenda or canon. See, for example, Allen W. Phillips's analysis of the poet's writings on *modernismo* (p. 135), the third of Juan Larrea's lectures in *Rubén Darío y la nueva cultura americana* (p. 78), and Enrique Anderson Imbert's references to the importance of Darío's "Los colores del estandarte" and "Palabras liminares" (*La originalidad de Rubén Darío*, p. 69).

2. Needless to say, in touting the aesthetic inaccessibility of his books, Darío does not discriminate between the acquisitive powers of the bourgeoisie and those of the oligarchies, since the possession of unique *objets d'art* corresponds to the impetus on the part of both socioeconomic groups to emblematize their material worth. This appeal to both groups can perhaps shed some light on the reasons why the Bourgeois King in Darío's short story is a king at all.

3. Among critics of Spanish American *modernismo*, assessments of the movement's attitude toward the mechanical production of art continue to be debated. According to Ramos, the exterior for these artists is the "lugar de la máquina amenazante" (p. 158). Jitrik makes a different assertion. In his perception of the *modernistas*' attitude, he valorizes the machine positively: "la originalidad es la instancia del 'invento', concepto que de ninguna manera es antagónica de la máquina sino, en el mundo moderno, complementario" [originality is the instance of "invention," a concept that in no way is antagonistic to the machine but, in the modern world, complementary] (p. 83).

Also see Gwen Kirkpatrick's article, "Technology and Violence: Casal, Darío, Lugones," *MLN* 102 (1987) 347–57.

4. Also, in the prologue to *Cantos de vida y esperanza*, Darío reiterates the exclusivity of the intellectual aristocracy to which he belongs. In an interesting fusion of racial and social categories with intellectual poverty and bad taste, the poet writes: "Mi respeto por la aristocracia del pensamiento, por la nobleza del arte, siempre es lo mismo. Mi antiguo aborrecimiento a la mediocridad, a la mulatez intelectual, a la chatura estética apenas si se aminora hoy con una razonada indiferencia" [My respect for the aristocracy of thought, for the nobility of art, is always the same. My former hatred of mediocracy, intellectual mulattoness, of aesthetic brutishness hardly lessens today with reasoned indifference] (p. 9). Although remarks such as these provide fascinating material for the study of nineteenth-century Spanish American conceptions of ethnicity, they also indicate the extent to which race and ethnicity, as we speak about them today, could not constitute a field of agency.

5. In my analysis, I cite Portuondo's essay and the articles on Casal by José Martí, Enrique José Varona, Rubén Darío, M. Márquez Sterling, and Pedro Henríquez Ureña from the first in the three-volume series of the poet's prose that Cuba's Consejo Nacional de Cultura published in 1963 to mark the centenary of Casal's birth. All citations of these authors are taken from this volume.

6. It should be clarified, however, that this distinction between Martí and Casal is greatest in the criticism on their poetry. By contrast, in a number of pieces from his column in *La Habana Elegante*, "La sociedad de la Habana," Casal ridicules important Spanish colonial officials and their *integrista* supporters. In the eyes of critics like José Antonio Portuondo (in Casal, *Prosas*, pp. 56–62) and Cintio Vitier, this journalism qualified the poet to be regarded as, in Vitier's words, "un separatista de sentimiento, no de acción"[a separatist of feeling, not of action] (in Casal, *Prosas*, p. 95).

Chapter 3

1. For easy reference, the entire poem is reproduced in the Appendix.

2. I am not suggesting that Darío and other *modernistas* participated in fascist politics. Such a statement would be historically inaccurate. Nonetheless, it must be pointed out that the literary movement promoted nationalisms and pan-Hispanism through the invocation of a unique and pure *raza*. This call for purity is not peculiar to nineteenth-century Spanish American cultural politics. Referring to the "pan-ic developments of nationalism (Pan-Slavism, Pan-Germanism,

Pan-Turanianism, Pan-Arabism, Pan-Americanism . . .)," Etienne Balibar and Immanuel Wallerstein argue that "racism constantly induces an excess of 'purism' as far as the nation is concerned: for the nation to be itself, it has to be racially or culturally pure" (pp. 59–60). The reference to the fasces in this poem has more to do with the call for a consensus on the construction of a pan-Hispanic community than for the physical elimination of groups that later came to be almost universally associated with twentieth-century fascism.

3. Triptolemus, according to the *Diccionario enciclopédico hispanoamericano*, is responsible for three inventions: the plow, agriculture, and, by extension, European civilization.

4. Whitman is a sustained presence not only for the *modernistas* but also for such important Spanish American poets as Pablo Neruda and Octavio Paz. For more information on this comparison, consult Enrico Mario Santí, "The Accidental Tourist: Walt Whitman in Latin America," in *Do the Americas Have a Common Literature?* ed. Gustavo Pérez Firmat (Durham: Duke University Press, 1990), pp. 156–76.

5. Octavio Paz refers to this poem as the "evangelio de la oligarquía hispanoamericana de fines de siglo" because it encourages ideas such as peace, industry, cosmopolitanism, and "latinidad," the watchwords of a faith in the progress and virtue of European immigration (*Cuadrivio*, p. 54).

Chapter 4

1. Over the last three centuries, *The Tempest* has been reworked and reelaborated on the basis of this theme. For a brief summary of these appropriations and further bibliography on the subject, consult Stephen Orgel's introduction to Shakespeare's play. In Latin American literary history, two prominent essays – Rodó's *Ariel* and Roberto Fernández Retamar's *Calibán: Apuntes sobre la cultura en nuestra América* (Mexico, D.F.: Editorial Diógenes, 1974) – offer radically different interpretive approaches to the construction of a Latin American identity. Both texts allegorize Ariel's and Calibán's individual response to each one's submission to labor as antagonism toward distinct forms of imperialism. Calibán's oppression under his master's magic (ideology) has made him an ideal protagonist in most readings of the colonial and postcolonial conditions.

2. Ernest Renan (1823–1892) is widely quoted in Rodó's essay. Among his several books, the most famous was *Vie de Jésus* (1863). For more detailed information on Renan and the historical contexts of his publications, see H. W. Wardman, *Ernest Renan: A Critical Biography* (London: University of London, 1964). Although Rodó never men-

tions Renan's play in *Ariel,* his appreciation for the works of the French scholar is evident in his frequent reference to Renan's ideas. Renan was also read by other Spanish American intellectuals. In 1893, Manuel González Prada wrote an essay reviewing the achievements of the recently deceased French thinker. In it, González Prada alludes to Renan in a fashion that resonates in Rodó's essay: "Renan fué poeta emparedado en la erudición o un Ariel que llevó en sus alas al polvo de una biblioteca" [Renan was a poet confined to erudition or an Ariel that carried the dust of a library on its wings] (p. 152).

3. These discourses and their polarization also constitute the literary commonplaces of civilization and barbarism and urban versus rural in nineteenth-century Hispanic letters. For an excellent study of these discourses in Spanish American letters, see Julio Ramos, *Desencuentros de la modernidad en América Latina,* especially the chapters entitled "Saber del otro: Escritura y oralidad en el Facundo de D. F. Sarmiento" and "Fragmentación de la república de las letras."

4. For instance, one of the chapters in Martínez Durán's book is called "Nueva invocación a Ariel. Magisterio espiritual permanente." The conclusion is entitled "Invocación final." Another example of this reinvocation is Hugo Torrano's *Rodó: Acción y libertad. Restauración de su imagén* (Montevideo: Barreiro y Ramos, 1973). Torrano's book, as one of its cover leaves indicates, unanimously won a UNESCO-sponsored contest in 1971 marking the centenary of Rodó's birth.

5. Angel Rama also points out this practice in the case of Darío's *Los raros* and *Prosas profanas* (*Los poetas modernistas en el mercado económico,* p. 8).

6. The movement from text to reality is a process that Miguel de Unamuno also employs in *Vida de don Quijote y Sancho* , a novel he published in 1905 (reprint, ed. Alberto Navarro, Madrid: Cátedra, 1988). He promotes don Quijote as a Spanish cultural figure and a life force greater than Cervantes, who, he suggests, is no more than a transcriber of the character's story.

7. This attenuation may be due to the formulaic courtesy that the literary politics of this correspondence required. Nonetheless, Rodríguez Monegal defends the integrity of Rodó and his work by offering the following explanation for the difference in tones between Unamuno's letters to Alas and to Rodó: "Para entender adecuadamente este juicio de Unamuno sobre *Ariel* – que no difiere en su esencia, aunque sí en el tono con el comunicado directamente a Rodó – hay que advertir que toda la larga carta en que se halla inserto incidentalmente, denuncia un estado de aguda tensión nerviosa, de insatisfacción y hasta de celos motivado por el silencio de Alas. . . . El tono con que se refiere a Rodó depende más de esa inquietud e inestabilidad emocional que de una profunda reflexión" [To under-

stand Unamuno's judgment of *Ariel* adequately – which does not differ in essence, although it does in tone from the one directly communicated to Rodó – one must be aware that the whole long letter in which it is to be found incidentally reveals a state of acute nervous tension, of dissatisfaction and even of jealousy motivated by Alas's silence. . . . The tone with which he refers to Rodó depends more on this worry and emotional instability than on profound reflection] (p. 1378).

8. Just as Alas's letter to Rodó became a prologue to *Ariel*, Valera's first letter to Darío on *Azul* (October 22, 1888) also introduces the text. See, for example, the Zig-Zag edition of *Azul* (Santiago de Chile, 1967).

9. Brotherston reports that Rodó attempted to counter the use of *Ariel* as an indictment of the United States: "As edition succeeded edition, the crude antithesis – Ariel (Latin America) *versus*, and superior to, Calibán (the U.S.A.) – was ascribed more and more to Rodó's essay. The reason for this lay entirely outside the work itself: indeed it is possible to account for much of *Ariel*'s success in terms of the atmosphere of the time, and the currents of feeling which still run strong in Latin America today" (p. 10).

Chapter 5

1. See Juan Loveluck's edition of *Azul* (Santiago de Chile: Editora Zig-Zag, 1967).

2. Also, Monguió, "La modalidad peruana del modernismo," and Arrieta, "El modernismo 1893–1900," list several reviews that were instrumental for the literary movement's momentum and the construction of Peruvian and Argentine national identities. I designate as *modernista* literary reviews those journals, reviews, and magazines that were founded in the last two decades of the past century. This chronological limitation derives not from my belief in the accuracy of this periodization but from their creators' awareness that the literature in the publications belonged to a specific cultural and regional movement. Guillermo Korn lists some of these reviews: "Las otras revistas [apart from Caracas' *El Cojo Ilustrado* (1892–1915)] que registran el movimiento modernista en América hispana son: *La Habana Elegante* (1883–1896) en Cuba, *Revista Azul* (1894–1896) y *Revista Moderna* en México. *Revista Nacional de Literatura y Ciencias Sociales* (1857–1897) en Montevideo, *Revista de América* (1896) de Rubén Darío y Jaimes Freyre y *El Mercurio de América* (1898–1900), ambas de Buenos Aires. *La Biblioteca* (1896–1898), publicada por Paul Groussac en Buenos Aires, acota en reseñas críticas la marcha del movimiento literario

modernista" (pp. 6–7). I will add to this list the Cuban review *La Habana Literaria*, which was launched in 1891 and I support Rodríguez Monegal's statement that the *Revista Nacional de Literatura y Ciencias Sociales* was founded by Rodó and his colleagues in 1895 and not in 1857 as Korn indicates. Because of the difficulty of locating and cataloguing these reviews, this list can only be partial.

3. Anderson analyzes the "old-fashioned novel" as a "structure" that may be created through a matrix of the vicissitudes of characters A, B, C, and D over a period of time (pp. 30–1). He also produces figures to show that there was a relationship between the number of books published and the "imagined linkage" that informs his notion of simultaneity (p. 38). For a detailed critique of Anderson's view of narrative, see Bhabha, pp. 308–11.

4. In "Le Paradoxe institutionel du manifeste," Anne-Marie Pelletier alludes to the same "prefiguring" of a collectivity and argues that the manifesto designates a particular type of sociolinguistic economy (p. 22). For a brief overview of the critical approaches to the manifesto, see Claude Abastado's "Introduction à l'analyse des manifestes." This article was one of several devoted to the manifesto in the October 1980 volume of *Littérature*. In 1983, *L'Esprit Créateur* published an issue subtitled *The Injunctive Text/Ecriture manifestaire*, in which Alice Yaeger Kaplan reviews recent theoretical work on manifestos (pp. 74–82). Although many of the critics I cite here proceed on the assumption that the manifesto is a literary genre of some kind or an act, praxis, or performance that may sometimes be inscribed, they have not been able to offer conclusive evidence that the manifesto can be characterized as a genre. "The gap between the manifestoes and the learned articles," Paul de Man writes commenting on nineteenth-century lyric, "has narrowed to the point where some manifestoes are quite learned and some articles – though by no means all – are quite provocative" ("Literary History and Literary Modernity," p. 144). In this study, I do not participate in the debate over the manifesto's generic characteristics. However, the uncanny resemblance between what these critics describe as a manifesto and what Jameson and others have termed the dialectic between ideology and utopia makes it an easy task to collapse these attempts to define generic properties into the discussion of that dialectic. My approach to *modernista* manifestos stresses their ideological content. In this regard, I make use of Pelletier's claim that the manifesto is simultaneously activated by two tenses: "celui de l'évocation critique et celui de la projection utopique, l'entre-deux dessinant le moment propre du manifeste: celui d'une prise de conscience mobilisatrice visant à promouvoir l'action" [that of a critical evocation and that of a utopian projection, the in-between laying out the manifesto's own

moment: that of a mobilizing consciousness aiming to promote action] (p. 18). Also useful is Marjorie Perloff's study on Marinetti's art of manifesto writing, "Violence and Precision: The Manifesto as Art Form." For an accessible compilation of some Latin American literary manifestos, consult Hugo J. Verani, *Las vanguardias literarias en Hispanoamérica: Manifiestos, proclamas y otros escritos* (Roma: Bulzoni Editore, 1986).

5. The range of mutually compensatory agreements – almost a review for every whim, which would help to explain the brief lives of many reviews at that time (see Fogelquist, "Helios, voz de un renacimiento hispánico," p. 334) – illustrates the variety of potential arrangements or contracts that these reviews tried to make with their readers.

6. After a declaration of intentions, *La Habana Literaria*'s manifesto also states: "Con tales propósitos, y la firme voluntad de realizarnos, llegamos a la arena periodística, solicitando el aprecio del público, y esperando encontrar en todos nuestros colegas (a quienes cordialmente saludamos) igual cortesía e idénticas consideraciones, a las que prometemos observar respecto a ellos en nuestras mutuas relaciones" [With such aims, and the firm will to self-realization, we come to the journalistic arena, soliciting the public's appreciation, and hoping to find in our colleagues (whom we cordially greet) the same courtesy and identical considerations, as those that we promise to observe with respect to them in our mutual relations] (p. 2). This call for common courtesy is formulaic and thereby reminiscent of Enzensberger's description of the relationship between the artist, the patron, and the eulogy.

7. José Luis Rivarola argues that "we" is an indexical that camouflages an "I" (p. 206). Lyons also states that "*we* is not 'the plural of I'" – that is, it is an "I" in addition to others over whom it is still the principal subject (p. 277).

8. For a more general treatment of this topos in Darío's writings, consult Barbara E. Kurtz, "'En el país de las alegorías: Alegorización en la poesía de Rubén Darío," *Revista Iberoamericana* 137 (1986): 875–93. Also see Joel Fineman, "The Structure of Allegorical Desire," *Allegory and Representation*, ed. Stephen J. Greenblatt (Baltimore: The Johns Hopkins University Press, 1981), pp. 26–60.

9. Similarly, in *Cosmopolis*' first issue, Pedro Coll et al. enthusiastically state: "emprenderemos la ruta de las meritorias peregrinaciones" [we will undertake the path of worthy pilgrimages] (p. 5).

Chapter 6

1. Sommer is astutely aware of her critical approach and of her personal/professional attitudes toward the Boom writers. In "Irresistible

Romance," she observes: "Paradoxically, the more the Boom pro-
tested indifference to tradition, the more it would send me back to
the persistent attractions that caused so much resistance. What was
it, I would ask, about earlier Latin American novels that provoked so
much resistance and denial?" (p. 72).

2. Naturally, this response is partial and not representative of an entire
people. Brennan notes that nationalism "is an ideology that, even in
its earliest forms in the nineteenth century, implied unequal development" (p. 59).

Bibliography of works cited

Abastado, Claude. "Introduction à l'analyse des manifestes." *Littérature* [Les Manifestes] 39.3 (1980): 3–11.

Alas, Leopoldo. *Los prólogos de Leopoldo Alas*, ed. David Torres. Madrid: Editorial Playor, 1984.

Alberdi, Juan Bautista, Roberto J. Payró, et al. *El escritor y la industria cultural: El camino hacia la profesionalización 1810–1900*, ed. Jorge B. Rivera. Buenos Aires: Centro Editor de América Latina, 1980.

Althusser, Louis. "Ideology and Ideological State Apparatuses (Notes Toward an Investigation)." In *Lenin and Philosophy and Other Essays*, trans. Ben Brewster, pp. 127–86. New York: Monthly Review Press, 1971.

"Preface to *Capital*, Volume One." In *Lenin and Philosophy and Other Essays*, trans. Ben Brewster, pp. 71–101. New York: Monthly Review Press, 1971.

Anderson, Benedict. *Imagined Communities: Reflection on the Origin and Spread of Nationalism*. London: Verso, 1983.

Anderson-Imbert, Enrique. *La originalidad de Rubén Darío*. Buenos Aires: Centro Editor de América Latina, 1967.

"Los poemas cívicos de 1905." In *Modernismo y 98*, ed. José Carlos Mainer, pp. 172–6. Historia y crítica de la literatura española. Barcelona: Editorial Crítica, 1980.

Appadurai, Arjun. "Disjuncture and Difference in the Global Cultural Economy." *Public Culture* 2.2 (1990): 1–24.

Armas, Emilio de. *Casal*. La Habana: Editorial Letras Cubanas, 1981.

Ashcroft, Bill, Gareth Griffiths, and Helen Tiffin. *The Empire Writes Back: Theory and Practice in Post-Colonial Literatures*. London: Routledge, 1989.

Balibar, Etienne, and Immanuel Wallerstein. *Race, Nation, Class: Ambiguous Identities*, trans. Etienne Balibar and Chris Turner. London: Verso, 1991.

Barrett, Michèle. "The Place of Aesthetics in Marxist Criticism." In *Marxism and the Interpretation of Culture*, ed. Cary Nelson and

Lawrence Grossberg, pp. 697–713. Urbana: University of Illinois Press, 1988.

Benjamin, Walter. *Charles Baudelaire: A Lyric Poet in the Era of High Capitalism*, trans. Harry Zohn. London: NLB, 1973.

"The Work of Art in the Age of Mechanical Reproduction." In *Illuminations*, trans. Harry Zohn, ed. Hannah Arendt, pp. 217–51. New York: Shocken Books, 1969.

Benston, Kimberly W. "Being There: Performance as Mise-en-Scène, Abscene, Obscene, and Other Scene." *PMLA* 107.3 (1992): 434–49.

Bhabha, Homi K. "DissemiNation: Time, Narrative, and the Margins of the Modern Nation." In *Nation and Narration*, ed. Homi K. Bhabha, pp. 291–322. London: Routledge, 1990.

Brennan, Timothy. "The National Longing for Form." In *Nation and Narration*, ed. Homi K. Bhabha, pp. 44–70. London: Routledge, 1990.

Brotherston, Gordon. *Latin American Poetry: Origins and Presence*. Cambridge University Press, 1975.

"La poesía andaluza y modernista de Manuel Machado." In *Actas del Congreso Internacional sobre el modernismo español e hispanoamericano*, ed. Guillermo Carnero, pp. 267–76. Córdoba: Imprenta San Pablo, 1987.

Carter, Boyd G. "La 'Revista Azul.' La resurrección fallida: Revista azul de Manuel Caballero." In *El modernismo*, ed. Lily Litvak, pp. 337–58. Madrid: Taurus, 1975.

Casal, Julián del. *Julián del Casal: Prosas*, Vol. 1. La Habana: Consejo Nacional de Cultura, 1963.

Castillo, Homero. Introduction. *Estudios críticos sobre el modernismo*, pp. 7–9. Madrid: Editorial Gredos, 1968.

Coll, Pedro, Pedro César Dominici, and L. M. Urbaneja Archepohl. "Charloteo." *Cosmópolis* 1.1 (1894): 1–5.

Concha, Jaime. *Rubén Darío*. Madrid: Ediciones Júcar, 1975.

Connerton, Paul. *How Societies Remember*. Cambridge University Press, 1989.

Darío, Rubén. *Autobiografía*. Vol. 15 of *Obras completas*. Madrid: Editorial Mundo Latino, 1918.

Azul, ed. Juan Loveluck M. Santiago de Chile: Editora Zig-Zag, 1967.

Canto a la Argentina. Vol. 9 of *Obras completas*. Madrid: Editorial Mundo Latino, 1918.

El canto errante. Vol. 16 of *Obras completas*. Madrid: Editorial Mundo Latino, 1918.

"El rey burgués." In *Azul . . ., El salmo de la pluma, Cantos de vida y esperanza, otros poemas*, ed. Antonio Oliver Belmás, pp. 17–20. México, D.F.: Editorial Porrúa, 1981.

Cantos de vida y esperanza. Vol. 7 of *Obras completas*. Madrid: Editorial Mundo Latino, 1918.

Poesías completas, ed. Luis Alberto Ruiz. Buenos Aires: Ediciones Antonio Zamora, 1967.

Prosas profanas. Vol. 2 of *Obras completas*. Madrid: Editorial Mundo Latino, 1917.

Darío, Rubén, and Ricardo Jaimes Freyre. *La Revista de América* (facsimile), ed. Boyd G. Carter. Managua: Comisión Nacional para la Celebración del Centenario del Nacimiento de Rubén Darío, 1967.

de Man, Paul. "Literary History and Literary Modernity." In *Blindness and Insight: Essays in the Rhetoric of Contemporary Criticism*, 2d ed., pp. 142–65. Minneapolis: University of Minnesota Press, 1983.

"Lyric and Modernity." In *Blindness and Insight: Essays in the Rhetoric of Contemporary Criticism*, 2d ed., pp. 166–86. Minneapolis: University of Minnesota Press, 1983.

Eagleton, Terry. "Nationalism: Irony and Commitment." In *Nationalism, Colonialism, and Literature*, ed. Seamus Deane, pp. 21–39. Minneapolis: University of Minnesota Press, 1990.

Ellis, Keith. *Critical Approaches to Rubén Darío*. Toronto: University of Toronto Press, 1974.

Enzensberger, Hans Magnus. "Poetry and Politics." In *The Consciousness Industry: On Literature, Politics and the Media*, pp. 62–82. New York: The Seabury Press, 1974.

Fogelquist, Donald F. "Helios, voz de un renacimiento hispánico." In *El modernismo*, ed. Lily Litvak, pp. 327–35. Madrid: Taurus, 1975.

"El carácter hispánico del modernismo." In *Estudios críticos sobre el modernismo*, ed. Homero Castillo, pp. 66–74. Madrid: Editorial Gredos, 1968.

Franco, Jean. "Criticism and Literature within the Context of a Dependent Culture." Paper presented at the Conference on Ideology and Latin America. New York University, IberoAmerican Language and Area Center, New York, April 29, 1975.

"Cultura y crisis." *Nueva Revista de Filología Hispánica* 35.2 (1987): 411–24.

Freud, Sigmund. *Civilization and Its Discontents*, ed. James Strachey. New York: W.W. Norton, 1961. Originally published 1930.

García Canclini, Néstor. "Contradicciones latinoamericanas: ¿Modernismo sin modernización?" In *¿Qué es el modernismo?: Nueva encuesta, nuevas lecturas*, ed. Richard A. Cardwell and Bernard McGuirk, pp. 371–8. Boulder, Colo.: Society of Spanish and Spanish-American Studies, 1993.

Gicovate, Bernardo. "Antes del modernismo." In *Estudios críticos sobre el modernismo*, ed. Homero Castillo, pp. 190–202. Madrid: Editorial Gredos, 1968.

Gleize, Jean-Marie. "Manifestes, préfaces: Sur quelques aspects du prescriptif." *Littérature* [Les Manifestes] 39.3 (1980): 12–16.

González, Aníbal. *Journalism and the Development of Spanish American Narrative.* Cambridge University Press, 1993.

La crónica modernista hispanoamericana. Madrid: José Porrúa Taranzas, 1983.

González Echevarría, Roberto. "The Case of the Speaking Statue: *Ariel* and the Magisterial Rhetoric of the Latin American Essay." In *The Voice of the Masters: Writing and Authority in Modern Latin American Literature,* pp. 8–32. Austin: University of Texas Press, 1985.

González Prada, Manuel. "Renan." In *Páginas libres,* pp. 137–52. Lima: Ediciones Nuevo Mundo, 1964.

Goodrich, Diana Sorensen. "Azul . . .: Los contextos de lectura." *Hispamérica* 40 (1985): 3–14.

Groussac, Paul. "La Biblioteca." *La Biblioteca* 1.1 (1896): 5–8.

Gullón, Ricardo. *Direcciones del modernismo.* Madrid: Editorial Gredos, 1971.

"Indigenismo y modernismo." In *Estudios críticos sobre el modernismo,* ed. Homero Castillo, pp. 267–78. Madrid: Editorial Gredos, 1968.

"La polémica entre modernismo y Generación del '98." In *Actas del Congreso Internacional sobre el modernismo español e hispanoamericano,* ed. Guillermo Carnero, pp. 69–81. Córdoba: Imprenta San Pablo, 1987.

Gutiérrez Nájera, Manuel, and Carlos Díaz Dufóo. "Al pie de la escalera." *Revista Azul* 1.1 (1894): 1–2.

Hernández Miyares, Enrique, and Alfredo Zayas. "Al Público." *La Habana Literaria* 1.1 (1891): 1–2.

Holquist, Michael. "The Politics of Representation." In *Allegory and Representation,* ed. Stephen J. Greenblatt, pp. 163–83. Baltimore: Johns Hopkins University Press, 1981.

Iser, Wolfgang. *The Act of Reading: A Theory of Aesthetic Response.* Baltimore: Johns Hopkins University Press, 1978.

Jameson, Fredric. "Conclusion: The Dialectic of Utopia and Ideology." In *The Political Unconscious: Narrative as a Socially Symbolic Act,* pp. 281–99. Ithaca: Cornell University Press, 1981.

"Versions of a Marxist Hermeneutic." In *Marxism and Form,* pp. 60–159. Princeton, N.J.: Princeton University Press, 1971.

Jauss, Hans Robert. *Toward an Aesthetic of Reception,* trans. Timothy Bahti. Minneapolis: University of Minnesota Press, 1982.

Jiménez, José Olivio. "José Martí y la creación del Modernismo hispanoamericano." In *Actas del Congreso Internacional sobre el modernismo español e hispanoamericano,* ed. Guillermo Carnero, pp. 203–18. Córdoba: Imprenta San Pablo, 1987.

Jitrik, Noé. *Las contradicciones del modernismo: Producciones poéticas y situaciones sociológicas.* México, D.F.: El Colegio de México, 1978.

Johnson, Barbara. "Poetry and Its Double: Two Invitations au voyage." In *The Critical Difference: Essays in the Contemporary Rhetoric of Reading*, pp. 23–51. Baltimore: Johns Hopkins University Press, 1980.

Kaplan, Alice Yaeger. "Review Article: Recent Theoretical Work with Pamphlets and Manifestoes." *L'Esprit Créateur* 23.4 (1983): 74–82.

Kirkpatrick, Gwen. *The Dissonant Legacy of Modernismo: Lugones, Herrera y Reissig, and The Voices of Modern Spanish American Poetry*. Berkeley: University of California Press, 1989.

Korn, Guillermo. *Obra y gracia de "El Cojo Ilustrado" de Caracas*. Caracas: Instituto de Investigaciones de Prensa, 1967.

Kronik, John. "Influencias francesas en la génesis del modernismo: Parnaso y simbolismo." In *Actas del Congreso Internacional sobre el modernismo español e hispanoamericano*, ed. Guillermo Carnero, pp. 35–51. Córdoba: Imprenta San Pablo, 1987.

Laclau, Ernesto. *New Reflections on the Revolution of Our Time*. London: Verso, 1990.

Laclau, Ernesto, and Chantal Mouffe. *Hegemony and Socialist Strategy: Towards a Radical Democratic Politics*. London: Verso, 1985.

Larrea, Juan. *Rubén Darío y la nueva cultura americana*. Valencia: Pre-Textos, 1987.

Litvak, Lily, ed. *El modernismo*. Madrid: Taurus, 1975.

Lugo-Ortiz, Agnes. "Escritura, nación y patriciado: Los 'Bustos' de Julián del Casal." *Revista de Estudios Hispánicos* 26.3 (1992): 391–412.

Lyons, John. *Introduction to Theoretical Linguistics*. Cambridge University Press, 1971.

Marcuse, Herbert. "The Affirmative Character of Culture." In *Negations: Essays in Critical Theory*, trans. Jeremy J. Shapiro, pp. 88–133. Boston: Beacon Press, 1968.

Martí, José. "Oscar Wilde." In *Prosa escogida*, ed. José Olivio Jiménez, pp. 59–70. Madrid: Editorial Magisterio Español, 1975.

Martínez Durán, Carlos. *José Enrique Rodó. En el espíritu de un tiempo y en la conciencia de América*. Caracas: Universidad Central de Venezuela, 1974.

Marx, Karl. *The Marx–Engels Reader*, ed. Robert C. Tucker. 2d ed. New York: W.W. Norton, 1978.

Molloy, Sylvia. "Conciencia del público y conciencia del yo en el primer Darío." *Revista Iberoamericana* 108–9 (1979): 443–57.

"Ser/Decir: Tácticas de un autorretrato." In *Essays on Hispanic Literature in Honor of Edmund L. King*, ed. Sylvia Molloy and Luis Fernández Cifuentes, pp. 187–99. London: Tamesis, 1983.

Monguió, Luis. "De la problemática del modernismo: La crítica y el 'cosmopolitismo'." In *Estudios críticos sobre el modernismo*, ed. Homero Castillo, pp. 254–66. Madrid: Editorial Gredos, 1968.

"Sobre la caracterización del modernismo." In *Estudios críticos sobre el modernismo,* ed. Homero Castillo, pp. 10–22. Madrid: Editorial Gredos, 1968.

Nietzsche, Friedrich. "On the Uses and Disadvantages of History for Life." In *Untimely Meditations,* trans. R. J. Hollingdale, pp. 57–123. Cambridge University Press, 1990.

Olivencia, Manuel. "Discursos de clausura del congreso." In *Actas del Congreso Internacional sobre el modernismo español e hispanoamericano,* ed. Guillermo Carnero, pp. 477–9. Córdoba: Imprenta San Pablo, 1987.

Ordiz Vásquez, F. Javier. "La esperanza del apocalipsis en la poesía de Rubén Darío."*Hora de Poesía* 59–60 (1988): 7–15.

Oyuela, Calixto. "Asociaciones literarias." In *Estudios literarios,* Vol. 2, pp. 365–72. Buenos Aires: Academia Argentina de Letras, 1943.

Paz, Octavio. *Cuadrivio.* México, D.F.: Editorial Joaquín Mortiz, 1965.

"Traducción y metáfora." In *El modernismo,* ed. Lily Litvak, pp. 97–117. Madrid: Taurus, 1975.

Pelletier, Anne-Marie. "Le Paradoxe institutionel du manifeste." *Littérature* [Les Manifestes] 39.3 (1980): 17–22.

Perloff, Marjorie. "Violence and Precision: The Manifesto as Art Form." *Chicago Review* 34.2 (1984): 65–101.

Pérus, Françoise. *Literatura y sociedad en América Latina: El modernismo.* La Habana: Casa de las Américas, 1975.

Phillips, Allen W. "Rubén Darío y sus juicios sobre el modernismo." In *Estudios críticos sobre el modernismo,* ed. Homero Castillo, pp. 118–45. Madrid: Editorial Gredos, 1968.

Rama, Angel. *Los poetas modernistas en el mercado económico.* Montevideo: Universidad de la República, Facultad de Humanidades y Ciencias, 1967.

Rubén Darío y el modernismo: Circunstancia socioeconómica de un arte americano. Caracas: Ediciones de la Universidad de Venezuela, 1970.

Ramos, Julio. *Desencuentros de la modernidad en América Latina: Literatura y política en el siglo XIX.* México, D.F.: Tierra Firme, 1989.

Reed, W. L., and M. J. Bristow, eds. *National Anthems of the World.* Poole, U.K.: Blandford Press, 1985.

Renan, Ernest. *Caliban.* Paris: Calman Lévy, 1878.

"What is a Nation?" In *Nation and Narration,* ed. Homi K. Bhabha, pp. 8–22. London: Routledge, 1990.

Rivarola, José Luis. "Quién es nosotros." *Estudios de Lingüística* 2 (1984): 201–6.

Rivera, Jorge B., ed. *El escritor y la industria cultural: El camino hacia la profesionalización 1810–1900.* Buenos Aires: Centro Editor de América Latina, 1980.

Rodó, José Enrique. *Ariel*, ed. Gordon Brotherston. Cambridge University Press, 1967.

Obras completas, ed. Emir Rodríguez Monegal. Madrid: Aguilar, 1967.

Rotker, Susana. *La invención de la crónica*. Buenos Aires: Ediciones Letra Buena, 1992.

Salinas, Pedro. "El problema del modernismo en España, o un conflicto entre dos espíritus." In *Estudios críticos sobre el modernismo*, ed. Homero Castillo, pp. 23–34. Madrid: Editorial Gredos, 1968.

Schulman, Ivan A. "Hacia un discurso crítico del modernismo concebido como sistema." In *¿Qué es el modernismo?: Nueva encuesta, nuevas lecturas*, ed. Richard A. Cardwell and Bernard McGuirk, pp. 257–75. Boulder, Colo.: Society of Spanish and Spanish-American Studies, 1993.

"Reflexiones en torno a la definición del modernismo." In *Estudios críticos sobre el modernismo*, ed. Homero Castillo, pp. 325–57. Madrid: Editorial Gredos, 1968.

Shakespeare, William. *The Tempest*, ed. Stephen Orgel. Oxford: Clarendon Press, 1987.

Sharman, Adam. "Modernismo, positivismo y (des)herencia en el discurso de la historia literaria." In *¿Qué es el modernismo?: Nueva encuesta, nuevas lecturas*, ed. Richard A. Cardwell and Bernard McGuirk, pp. 319–38. Boulder, Colo.: Society of Spanish and Spanish-American Studies, 1993.

Silliman, Ron. "The Political Economy of Poetry." In *The New Sentence*, pp. 20–31. New York: Roof Books, 1977–85.

Sommer, Doris. "Irresistible Romance: The Foundational Fictions of Latin America." In *Nation and Narration.*, ed. Homi K. Bhabha, pp. 71–98. London: Routledge, 1990.

Valera, Juan. "Azul . . ." In Vol. 3 of *Obras completas*. Madrid: Aguilar, 1958.

Valle-Castillo, Jorge. Prologue to Rubén Darío, *Prosas políticas*. Managua: Publicaciones Ministerio de Cultura, 1982.

Vargas Vila, José María. *Rubén Darío*. Madrid: V. H. de Sanz Calleja, 1917.

Vidal, Hernán. *Sentido y práctica de la crítica literaria socio-histórica: Panfleto para la proposición de una arqueología acotada*. Minneapolis: Institute for the Study of Ideologies and Literature, 1984.

Žižek, Slavoj. "Beyond Discourse-Analysis." Appendix to Ernesto Laclau, *New Reflections on the Revolution of Our Time*, pp. 249–60. London: Verso, 1990.

Index